Contents

Island Emigrants

The Proceedings of a Conference held in the Isle of Harris, 10–12 September 2009

The Islands Book Trust

Published in 2010 by The Islands Book Trust

www.theislandsbooktrust.com

ISBN: 978-1-907443-02-2

British Library Cataloguing in Publication Data. A CIP record for this book can be obtained from the British Library.

Cover design by James Hutcheson

The Islands Book Trust, Ravenspoint Centre, Kershader, South Lochs, Isle of Lewis, HS2 9QA. Tel: 01851 880737

Typeset by Erica Schwarz. Printed by JF Print Limited, UK

Introduction and Conclusions

John Randall

Introduction

Emigration is a phenomenon which over the centuries has affected most families in the Outer Hebrides. It is still an important part of island life today, through the personal links with people of island descent all over the world. It was therefore a natural topic to select for the Book Trust's annual conference in 2009, Scotland's Year of Homecoming. This volume is based on contributions to the conference, and is a permanent memento of a very successful and memorable event.

The conference took place over three days in September 2009 in Leverburgh, South Harris. Like all Book Trust events, it was a conference with a difference, bringing together people from widely varied backgrounds to share experiences and learn from each other. We had some outstanding academic speakers, such as Tom Devine and Marjory Harper, and local scholars such as Bill Lawson and Roddy Balfour, all experts on aspects of the history of Scottish and island emigration. We also placed Hebridean emigration in a wider context through looking at the history of emigration from the west of Ireland through the eyes of Mícheál de Mórdha, Director of the Great Blasket Centre in County Kerry. This was combined with contributions from people with vivid first-hand experience of emigration, able to bring a personal and often emotional dimension to what was and is after all a life-changing experience for thousands of people. It was indeed a moving experience to hear the stories and feelings of returning emigrants, talking about their own or their family's memories, in a session ably chaired by Kenny MacIver.

It was this mixture which contributed so much to the success and enjoyment of the conference. In addition to the more formal sessions, we looked at films of emigration, enjoyed a ceilidh at which young musicians from Harris gave an unforgettable performance of songs of emigration, heard sound recordings about emigration from Margaret Bennett, Chris Lawson and Morag MacLeod, visited the exhibition about island emigration at the Seallam! Visitor Centre at Northton and undertook a tour of places affected by emigration in Harris led by Bill Lawson. A children's competition on the theme of emigration attracted more than fifty entries from schools from Lewis to South Uist, and the prizes were presented by Michael Russell MSP, Minister for Culture in the Scottish Government, who closed the conference.

The conference was based in the local communities of Leverburgh, Rodel, and Northton in South Harris, and this also added greatly to the enjoyment and sense of occasion. The Book Trust would like to thank everyone involved, particularly the Leverburgh Community Hall, Rodel Hotel, Seallam! Visitor Centre, and a host of volunteers, for making the event such an outstanding success. We would also like to thank our sponsors, Homecoming Scotland, Comhairle nan Eilean Siar, and Comunn na Gaidhlig; and Alison Kennedy, our Gaelic summer placement student, who took on much of the organisational burden.

Conclusions

It is an impossible and foolhardy task to attempt to summarise all the ideas, theories, and findings which emerged over the course of a stimulating three days. This is not the purpose of this brief opening chapter. I would commend all the contributions which appear in this volume as worthy of further study and consideration. Several of them, particularly Marjory Harper's very comprehensive and thoughtful closing chapter, and Bill Lawson's overview, are valuable and genuinely new contributions to an important ongoing discussion. The thoughts below are simply some personal reflections which may highlight some of the key issues:

- Certain themes associated with emigration tend to dominate popular understanding and over-shadow everything else. First amongst these is the Clearances. In many minds clearance and emigration are different sides of the same coin. But the story of emigration is far more complex and multi-faceted than this – witness Marjory Harper's insightful conclusions on different phases of island emigration, and Bill Lawson's masterly overview based on pioneering statistical research on families in the Outer Hebrides which demonstrates clearly that very different factors led to emigration at various times from the eighteenth century onwards.

- Of course, clearance was indeed the dominant force during certain periods, as Tom Devine brought out in his opening address. He referred particularly to the period 1849–1854, when the crisis of 'removal' of population, regarded by landlords as surplus to requirements in the wake of the downturn in demand for kelp and the ravages of the potato famine, was concentrated in the islands. The 'unbridled and uninhibited' recourse to clearance in the first part of the 1850s reflected the change of ownership of many estates following bankruptcy, the failure of relief measures in the earlier period, the prevalence of Malthusian population theories, racial stereotypes of Celtic people, and the traumatic experience of Ireland.

- During this period clearance was planned on some estates in great detail with individual selection of those deemed poorest, for example cottars or those in rent arrears, with moral judgements being made about the suitability of particular people.

- Another popular image of emigration is the deserted island, typified by twentieth century evacuations as in the case of St Kilda or the Great Blasket Island in Ireland, and characterised by feelings of great nostalgia and a sense of guilt for a lost culture. The sentimental song is perhaps the art form best fitted to portraying this image of loss.

- Interestingly, almost all the entries to the children's competition about emigration, whether poems in Gaelic or English, or paintings, focused on clearance and evacuation – the history of loss, victimisation, failure, and nostalgia. Powerful themes indeed!

- But we need to see these themes in the wider context of emigration from the islands over the last 250 years, as powerful but not necessarily representative episodes. Emigration affected some areas more than others (see for example Bill Lawson's figures indicating that many more people left South Uist between 1750 and 1900 than left Lewis); and the main destination areas changed noticeably over time – in chronological order Carolina, New York, Hudson's Bay, Prince Edward Island, Nova Scotia, Cape Breton, Quebec, Australia, Ontario, the Prairies, and South America. Each of these emigrations had particular characteristics, for example in terms of area of origin and religion; and by no means all of the emigrants were from the poorer levels of society, for example the tacksmen in the eighteenth century.

- An intriguing possibility to emerge from the contributions to the conference is that the overall pattern of emigration from the Outer Hebrides may be different from that of many or even most other parts of the Highlands and Islands, in that the balance seems over most of the last 250 years to have been weighted more towards overseas emigration rather than migration to the big cities of the Scottish central belt and England. In this respect, Hebridean emigration may be more analogous to the pattern of Irish emigration. And a possible explanation may be the central concern with land (rather than a paid job) in the Hebridean psyche. If getting access to land was the central concern, then clearly there were more opportunities in Canada than Glasgow in the nineteenth century.
- But of course, emigration from the islands to the mainland of the UK is a very significant part of island culture too, and has generated its own history, writings, memories, and songs over at least the last century, as demonstrated by Morag MacLeod in a wonderful after-dinner talk with mainly Gaelic recordings. Moreover, it is perhaps a dimension which has increased in recent decades with the spread of higher educational opportunities, overwhelmingly concentrated on the mainland.

- The conference also brought out the very different experiences of emigrants from the islands in their new areas of settlement. Where emigrants settled in communities, as in the Eastern Townships of Canada, or in Cape Breton, their culture as seen through religion and the Gaelic language was preserved much longer – as the recordings and contributions from Margaret Bennett and Chris Lawson evocatively illustrated. In other destination areas, noticeably Australia, emigrants tended to disperse and were integrated more quickly into the host society.

- But personal links with the island homeland can be preserved in a rich variety of ways. It is not only in the case of Barra and Cape Breton (a remarkable story memorably presented by Calum Macneil) that cultural links are maintained today. Greta Mackenzie's account of finding relatives in Patagonia, Tully McIntyre's homecoming from Seattle to Uist, and the stories of Norman MacRae and Annie MacRitchie linking Stornoway and Detroit bear vivid testimony to that.

- These links and the shared histories of communities across the world surely do represent tremendous opportunities, both economically and culturally, for Scotland and the Hebrides as they look to the future. The closing remarks by Michael Russell MSP, Minister for Culture in the Scottish Government, were certainly apposite and welcome. A shared history should be the basis for reappraisal and debate, rather than the unthinking perpetuation of conventional and often mythical stereotypes on both sides.

- The final discussion session of the conference spontaneously and encouragingly returned to this theme, and the issue of how far our own perceptions of island history perpetuate an image of victimisation, failure, and loss, which firstly may not be accurate and secondly may certainly not be the best mind-set for young people from the Hebrides as they try to come to terms with their future and that of their culture in the modern world. As Bill Lawson states, there is much to be proud of in the history of emigration from the islands and we should surely be seeking to present a balanced picture. Maybe an indication of progress would be if, in a future competition for children about emigration, there were some images of Hebridean pioneers and successes in the New World!

1

ꕤ

Human Selection, Clearance, and Emigration – The Western Highlands and Islands in the Nineteenth Century

Synopsis of paper presented by Professor Tom Devine

Professor Tom Devine of the University of Edinburgh opened the conference by setting out four key characteristics which define the Scottish Diaspora:

(a) Longevity – emigration from Scotland has been taking place for a very long time, as far back as the thirteenth and fourteenth centuries with the movement of some of its people to other parts of Europe.

(b) Volume – in the nineteenth century Scotland was the second richest country in the world yet, paradoxically, it topped the emigration league. There has been a high volume of emigrants from Scotland over the centuries.

(c) Global reach – emigration from Scotland has stretched well beyond Imperial destinations. The 'reach' of Scottish emigrants has been exceptionally long and wide, embracing South America, China, Japan, Africa, and so on.

(d) Complexity – the Scottish emigration story is extraordinarily complex, in part because of its longevity, volume, and global reach.

Diaspora, the scattering or dispersal of people, only applies to a few groups, such as the Irish, Chinese, and Palestinians, but includes the Scots.

In terms of Scottish Gaeldom and Diaspora, Sir Edward Pine Coffin predicted the 'extermination' of the people, because of the scale of emigration from the Highlands and Islands in the mid nineteenth century. He had been put in charge of famine relief in south-west Ireland in 1846 and had an unmatched understanding among Government officials of the problems of the so-called Celtic fringe of the British Isles.

Professor Devine described several distinctive features of the 1840s and 1850s emigration period from the Highlands and Islands:

(a) The longevity of the Highland crisis is important – the potato famine there lasted four years longer than in Ireland.

(b) There are very few other areas or time periods providing such rich material and information to enable the historian to discover and understand in depth what was happening.

(c) There was an unprecedented level of survey associated with emigration.

(d) The scale of newspaper coverage (both pro and anti emigration) is unprecedented.

(e) The sheer intensity of the removal is striking. For example, the island of Ulva had a population of around 600 in 1846, reduced to a mere sixteen by 1861. Lewis was experiencing evictions of around 1,000 to 1,200 people annually during the 1840s, which represents a ten-fold increase from the 1820s.

(f) In the 1840s and 1850s clearance was concentrated in the Inner and Outer Hebrides, not much on the mainland. This is because clearance had already taken place on a large scale on the mainland and the islands represented the last part of the process. The key period of clearance and emigration was 1849–1854. Some 80,000 people were affected. There is a strong link between clearance and emigration in the 1840s and 1850s. The norm was removal and expulsion rather than removal and resettlement or 'crowding in' elsewhere on an estate.

(g) The measures of callousness and inhumanity during the late 1840s and early 1850s are unprecedented. The behaviour of estates was meticulous, deploying a careful and systematic evaluation in deciding who should be removed or put into the cottar class on an estate. Professor Devine referred to this as a 'process of human selection'. There was a careful checklist of those to be removed. They included the poorest – those requiring to be fed, cottars, and the poorer tenant classes or those who might fall on to the Poor Law and have a devastating effect on the rates of estates. Moral judgements were made by estates in selecting individuals for clearance. Estates felt they had a new liberty to do this because to do so would not give them a bad name in London and 'society'. Those who belonged to kelp-burning communities were also selected for removal because they had become a redundant population following the collapse in the price of kelp.

(h) Famine was another contributory factor – a necessary but not sufficient cause in itself of removal and emigration. Clearance on a massive scale took place only from 1848 onwards and did not happen in 1845, 1846, or 1847 at the height of the famine.

Professor Devine explained four key reasons behind this great watershed in Highland history, a period marked by a loss of one-third of the area's population by 1861:

(a) Failure of relief efforts.

(b) The Highland land class had been rejuvenated by new money and there was therefore funding available to mount assistance for large scale emigration.

(c) Judicial force operated in favour of clearances.

(d) There was an uncritical orthodoxy amongst most newspapers and in other quarters. The orthodoxy was that the Highlands and Islands were over-populated and needed 'correcting'. In order to avoid the 'leprosy' of Ireland, more than 40,000 Gaels needed transporting. This was accompanied by a strong racial element of the Celt being inferior and the Anglo-Saxon superior and representing progress. There was an opportunity for the 'final settlement of the Gaelic problem' and for Germanic people to fill the gap which would be left by the Celts.

The Free Church lacked the civil authority and power to stop forced emigration. People were legally helpless – cottars and crofters who were two or more years in rent arrears did not have a legal leg to stand on. They were 'primitives who had to go to allow for progress'. The factorial class was often educated in Scottish universities and had a different work ethic and world view to the

> communities they were in charge of. The factors believed, with an intellectual passion, in what they were doing, seeing clearances as a positive mind-set to solve the problems of these areas. This is not to pardon what was done but simply to try to understand it. The Restitution Committees of 1846–1850 had poured the equivalent of millions of pounds into the area but the factors felt this was 'to no effect' because they thought the population was 'delinquent'. What the factors failed to realise was that the work of the Restitution Committees kept people alive. By the 1840s the cardinal social belief in middle and upper ranks was that 'people were poor because of their own causes', not because of environmental or any other reasons.

Professor Devine's keynote address therefore set out an overall context and some defining characteristics of Scottish and Highlands and Islands emigration, before concentrating in more detail on one particular period in the Western Highlands and Islands – the 1840s and 1850s. Other sessions at the conference looked at different periods, illustrating the great complexity of which Professor Devine had spoken.

2

ᘓ

Emigration from the West of Ireland – A Case Study of the Great Blasket Island

Mícheál de Mórdha

Firstly, I should brief you generally about emigration and how it has affected the Irish nation, especially during the last century and a half. Ever since the Great Famine (1845–1848), the island of Ireland has been haemorrhaging its population on a large scale, in the form of emigration. It is only very recently that this haemorrhaging has stopped.

Of course, emigration from Ireland did not spurt up suddenly as a consequence of the Famine, as people had been leaving the country for a long time before that, although on a smaller scale:

- Emigration (sometimes forced) from Ireland began in the pre-Christian era.

- Considerable (but untallied) numbers left Éire in the seventeenth and eighteenth centuries – for the continent and other British colonies in the western hemisphere.

- Convicts were 'transported' to 'penal colonies' in Australia from late in the eighteenth century in the hope none would return.
- Mass emigration occurred between the close of the Napoleonic wars and the beginning of World War One.
- Between 1801 and 1921 it is estimated that at least 8 million men, women and children left Ireland for good.[1]

From ancient times, people from my country have found themselves in various corners of this globe, for one reason or another. We have served in the armies of various countries over the centuries, with the British army being no exception. So, our Diaspora is all over the world.

On a global scale, an estimated population of some 70 million claim partial Irish descent, at least as part of their cultural heritage, according to a former *Uachtarán na hÉireann* (President) Mary Robinson, who spoke about this in December 1990.

Certain trends in Irish emigration have been identified:

- Prior to the Great Famine (1845–1848) emigrants tended to go to Canada as a final destination.
- Between the Famine and World War One the main destination tended to be the USA.
- Thereafter, Great Britain was the main destination as a general rule of thumb.

The preamble to a famous song by the Dubliners, *McAlpine's Fusiliers*, goes like this: '*'t was the year of '39, the sky was full of lead, Hitler was heading for Poland, and Paddy for Holyhead!*'

Destitution and oppression were two main reasons for emigrating from Ireland, but there were many more. From the middle of the eighteenth century the population of Ireland expanded at an unprecedented rate, due mainly to the fact that the simple potato became the staple diet of the populace. Then the potato famine occurred and mass starvation was the result.

It is estimated that in 1791 there were some 4.4 million people in the country. Population figures for other years are given below:

- 1821: 6.8 million
- 1831: 7.8 million
- 1841: 8.2 million (growth rate had slowed)
- 1851[2]: 6.5 million (famine and emigration).

In her seminal book on the Great Famine, *The Great Hunger*, Cecil Woodham-Smith declares:

> *It is however agreed by all authorities that about the year 1780 the population of Ireland began to take an extraordinary upward leap. The increase between 1779 and 1841 has been placed at the almost incredible figure of 172 per cent…*
>
> *By 1841, when a census was taken, the population had reached 8,175,124, and Disraeli declared that Ireland was the most densely populated country in Europe; on arable land, he asserted, the population was denser than that of China.*[3]

Awareness and acceptance of emigration as a method of seeking a better life increased exponentially after the devastation of the Famine and a pattern of heavy emigration continued for well over a century from the mid 1840s. This resulted in a severe decrease in the population, and by 1911 the whole island of Ireland (North and South) was home to around 4 million people. The Irish Free State was established by the end of 1922 and Northern Ireland opted out. The population of the Free State (Éire) was 3 million in 1926 and fell to 2.8 million in 1961.

Ireland's low population was causing great concern to the Government, especially when it was noticed that Northern Ireland's population was increasing slightly, from 1.25 million in 1926 to 1.4 million in 1956. The Government developed successful economic policies in the 1960s, under the legendary Taoiseach, Seán Lemass, and a gentle increase in population subsequently occurred. The population reached 3.5 million in 1986 and by then a brake was being applied to the general trend of heavy emigration, although a considerable number of young people had no option but to emigrate during the recessionary years of the late 1980s and the early 1990s.

We then witnessed the Celtic Tiger years, from 1995 to 2007, during which our economy prospered. By 2006 the population of Saorstát na hÉireann (Irish Free State) had reached 4.235 million – a remarkable turnabout in many ways.

As well as that, the number of immigrants, or people migrating into the country, outweighed the number of emigrants (people leaving or going out of the country). It was not until the Celtic Tiger years that Ireland became fully conversant with the general concept of population migration. Up until then it was mostly emigration (the outward migration of people) that interested us and, indeed, many people in this island thought that emigration affected our country more than any other and the 'curse of emigration' was uniquely Irish.

Sadly, emigration from this country is again[4] being contemplated by many of our young people, who have been rendered jobless by the current economic crisis which has enveloped the whole world in recent times. Countries in which Irish emigrants could traditionally find work – like the USA, Great Britain, European Union countries and the Antipodes – are also suffering from the economic downturn and having their own unemployment problems, so there are very few employment opportunities out there. Even Canada, which until very recently offered employment opportunities *go leor*, appears to be closing its doors to immigrants seeking employment.

The following report was placed on the website of the Irish Central Statistics Office[5] in September 2009:

> ***Resumption of net outward migration***
>
> *The number of emigrants from the State in the year to April 2009 is estimated to have increased by over 40% from 45,300 to 65,100, while the number of immigrants continued to decline over the same period, from 83,800 to 57,300.*
>
> *These combined changes have resulted in a return to net outward migration for Ireland (–7,800) for the first time since 1995.*
>
> *Over the same period, the number of births reached a new high of 74,500 (not seen since 1896) while the number of deaths was 29,400, resulting in strong natural growth for the year to April 2009 of 45,100.*
>
> *The combined effect of the natural increase and migration resulted in a population increase of 37,300 (+0.8%) bringing the population estimate to 4.46 million in April 2009.*

> *The main features of the 2009 figures are:*
>
> *Of the 65,100 people who emigrated in the year to April 2009, EU12 nationals were by far the largest group accounting for 30,100, with Irish nationals being the second largest at 18,400.*
>
> *Immigration of all non-Irish national groups showed a decline, with those from the EU12 countries showing the greatest fall from 33,700 in April 2008 to 13,500 in April 2009, a decline of 20,200.*

Table 2.1 details the migration pattern for Éire up to 2006. It is also to be found on the website of the Irish Central Statistics Office.

The figures clearly show that there was a net number of 46,000 immigrants to this country between 2002 and 2006 and that we lost 27,000 of our mainly young population to emigration during another economic crisis in the late 1980s. Some of these, of course, returned or immigrated into the country during the Celtic Tiger years.

After all these figures and facts we can zoom in on West Kerry[6] and the Great Blasket Island.

The maps (in the central plate section) show the location of the Great Blasket, or *An Blascaod Mór*, the main island in the Blasket archipelago.

The Great Blasket Island was a microcosm of the hundreds of remote communities which inhabited the west coast of Ireland up to 1950 or so. All these communities depended on subsistence farming and fishing to stay alive. What set the Great Blasket apart from the other communities is, of course, the extraordinary literary output of its community. There was also the fact that, although the island is only a couple of

Table 2.1: Average annual births, deaths, natural increase and estimated net migration for each intercensual period, 1926–2006 (thousands)

Period	Total births	Total deaths	Natural increase	Change in population	Estimated net migration
1926–1936	58	42	16	0	–17
1936–1946	60	43	17	–1	–19
1946–1951	66	40	26	1	–24
1951–1956	63	36	27	–12	–39
1956–1961	61	34	26	–16	–42
1961–1966	63	33	29	13	–16
1966–1971	63	33	30	19	–11
1971–1979	69	33	35	49	14
1979–1981	73	33	40	38	–3
1981–1986	67	33	34	19	–14
1986–1991	56	32	24	–3	–27
1991–1996	50	31	18	20	2
1996–2002	54	31	23	49	26
2002–2006	61	28	33	79	46

miles from the mainland, its inhabitants had to negotiate the treacherous Blasket Sound in order to get there and back.

Just as the island authors were turning the eyes of the world towards their remote island and its culture, the community there had entered its final phase – the population decline

Table 2.2: Analysis of Great Blasket population 1841–1950

Year	*Population*	*Male*	*Female*
1841	153	85 = 55.56%	68 = 44.44%
1851	97	47 = 48.45%	50 = 51.55%
1901	145	85 = 58.62%	60 = 41.38%
1911	160	88 = 55%	72 = 45%
1926	143	N/A	N/A
1936	110	64 = 58.18%	46 = 41.82%
1946	45[a]	32 = 71.11%	13 = 28.89%
1947	51	35 (2 male infants included) = 68.63%	16 = 31.37%
1950 (Márta)	30	23 (+ 1 male child) = 80%	6 = 20%

[a] Married – 10; single – 27; widows (male and female) – 8.

which resulted in the abandonment of the island in November 1953. An analysis of the population is given in Table 2.2.

The island never had more than 200 inhabitants. It appears that the island population reached its peak in 1916 when the main island author, Tomás Ó Criomhthain, stated that there were 'nine score' (i.e. 180) residents that year.

What is remarkable is the fact that the percentage of women in the community was always lower than that of men, except for the entry for 1851 (the first census after the Great Famine). By 1950, just three years before the abandonment, the population of the island was 80 per cent male and mostly single. The only way to explain this disproportionate gender balance is that more women than men chose to migrate from the island, especially from the 1930s onwards.

Going to live in the remote community on the island did not generally appeal to young women from the mainland (on receiving proposals of marriage from island families) and the same community may have been regarded as backward by some. Also, most of the young women of marriageable age who were born on the island did not wish to settle down in their own community. They preferred menial jobs as domestic servants in the towns and cities on the mainland. But a lot of them were not content with the employment opportunities on offer on the mainland either – and looked west to America for relief. The Great Blasket is sometimes called 'The next parish to America' as it is supposed to be the most westerly area in Ireland.

Quite a number of the island's young men also left for a better life in the USA or elsewhere. Some returned after a few years but most settled around the city of Springfield, in western Massachusetts. The following pattern appeared in almost all the island families. On reaching eighteen years or so, the eldest child in an island family would find, or be sent, the fare for a one way ticket from the port of Cobh (formerly Queenstown) in Cork to a destination in America, where close relatives would have already settled. An 'American Wake' would be held for the young person, as he or she would not be seen again on the island for many years. It was almost like a death in the family and the only hope was that the young person may return some day as a well heeled 'Yank', after making their fortune on the streets of Springfield. We have a report of one mother crying solidly for one whole week, after her daughter had emigrated.

The second child in the family would then receive the passage money – as soon as their eldest sibling, who was by now settled in America, could afford to send the money 'over'; or a relative might send the money, if it could be afforded. And so the pattern followed until there would only be one child left – usually male – who would remain on the island in order to care for his parents in old age. But that last remaining child would not be a good prospect for marriage – especially as he had elderly parents to care for.

One of the island's authors, Muiris Ó Súilleabháin, describes the prelude to an 'American Wake' on Great Blasket in the following passage:

> *Kate Peg was constantly coming to the house now and she and Maura talking of nothing but America. They would run across to the wall where pictures from Springfield were hanging. 'Oh,' Kate would say, 'we will go into that big building the first day, Maura.' Then the two of them would run out on the floor dancing for joy. 'You will send home pretty things to me?' said Eileen. 'We will, of course,' said Maura indifferently. Then Eileen too would dance over the floor.*
>
> *Three weeks later the passage money came.*
>
> *She was changed that evening, crying bitterly with the letter in her hands.*
>
> *'What is the good of crying so, you foolish girl?' said my father, who was sitting in his chair with a mournful look on him. Kate Peg came in, her eyes as red as the rose from weeping.*
>
> *'Well, Kate,' said my father, 'what news have you?'*
>
> *'I have none, save that the passage money came for me today. I hear Maura has hers too.'*

'She has,' said my father, 'and she has been distracted ever since.'

'Why are you crying so, Maura?' said Kate, raising her head. 'Didn't you see Nora Pats go, with no kinsfolk at all over there, the poor girl? And isn't it over there all your own people are?'

I noticed his cap far down over my father's eyes that evening as I had never seen it before. Eileen was in the far corner crying to herself.

'Faith, it is a fine prospect in store for you,' said my father with a long sigh, bending over the fire to put a live cinder in his pipe.

After a while Maura stopped crying, only a sob coming now and then as she put the kettle on the fire.

'Had the King any news when he came in, Kate?' asked my father, crossing his knees.

'I did not hear any except of the crowds that are going across to America this week.'

'God help the old people, there will be none to bury them with the haste that is on the world.'

'There's no doubt but there is a great change in the times.'

'Upon my soul, Kate, I remember when there was no thought of America any more than the chair I am sitting on, and they were fine happy days.'

Maura was crying every day now. 'Musha, I don't know in the world,' she would say when she washed the plates, 'will the day ever come when I will be washing these again.'

> *...Time was passing and the appointed day approaching. A mournful look was coming over the very walls of the house. The hill above the village which sheltered the houses seemed to be changing colour like a big, stately man who would bend his head in sorrow. The talk throughout the village was all of Maura and Kate going away...*[7]

It is evident that residents of the Dingle Peninsula were very much aware of life in America by the middle of the nineteenth century.[8] Even before that time, some residents from fishing communities in West Kerry went across the Atlantic on fishing expeditions to the great fishing bank of Newfoundland. A few even settled over there, never to return home. We have heard of one married man from this area, who went fishing to the Grand Banks, went ashore there, met a lady, got married and never returned to his original family on this side of the Atlantic!

We do not know when the first Blasket person decided to go to Springfield – but a lot of people followed suit – especially from the end of the nineteenth century. They were not only from the Great Blasket, but from the whole area of West Kerry. All around the country, there was a tradition of people emigrating from one particular place in Ireland to a particular city or destination in America. In our area, the tendency, especially in the latter years of the Blasket community's existence, was to go to Springfield or to its neighbouring big city – Hartford, in Connecticut. Some went as far as the mines of Butte, Montana and a few even went to the West Coast. The constant goal was employment and a better life. The sense of neighbourliness, practised in their native communities, was brought across to the 'New World'. So, they helped each other on 'the other side'.

Muiris Ó Súilleabháin, the author, also contemplated the emigrant's path, but was eventually persuaded by his friend, the great English scholar George Thomson, to join *An Garda Síochána*, the Irish police force.

I looked west at the edge of the sky where America should be lying and I slipped back on the paths of thought. It seemed to me now that the New Island was before me with its fine streets and great high houses, some of them so tall that they scratched the sky; gold and silver out on the ditches and nothing to do but to gather it.

I see the boys and the girls who were once my companions walking the street, laughing brightly and well contented. I see my brother Shaun and my sisters Maura and Eileen walking along with them and the talking together of me. The tears were rising in my eyes but I did not shed them.

As the old saying goes, 'bitter the tears that fall but more bitter the tears that fall not'.[9]

The following is an extract from the writings of the late Professor Tom Biuso, native of Springfield, Professor of English in Colby Sawyer College, New Hampshire. With his untimely death, his book remained unfinished:

Since the great potato famine of the 1840s … the Blasket Islands have had a much more intimate link with the west, with that next parish, in the form of the American city of Springfield, Massachusetts. Springfield, and the neighboring Connecticut Valley cities of Hartford, Connecticut and Holyoke, Massachusetts, seemed much nearer to them and their Island home than their own capital city of Dublin, or the cities of London and Liverpool, each of which attracted large numbers of Irish emigrants as permanent residents and migrant laborers. Today, Blasket-Americans conjecture that it was the building of railways which brought the first Islanders to Springfield. That might put them there in the 1830s or 1840s, but no trace of them then can be found. Today, an Islander in Holyoke with a long memory claims that the first Islander to come to the area was a Guiheen, and that he came before the Civil War.

Also, the role which kinship plays in emigration of the Islanders to Springfield cannot be underestimated. Whoever went first, they soon sent back for a brother or a sister, lending the passage money, and taking care of the initiation when the new arrival appeared on the steps of the old railway terminal on Main or Lyman Streets.

Thomas Moriarty, a man with West Kerry roots, is Professor Emeritus of History at Our Lady of the Elms College in Chicopee, western Massachusetts, a neighbouring city to Springfield. He describes early immigration to the Springfield area:

Springfield is a very old city; it dates from the 1630s and it included Chicopee…and Holyoke and West Springfield, all three of which are now separate cities…

By the middle of the 19th century Springfield had become a pretty significant area. They had begun to build canals for the mills that would be built along the banks of the canal. The mills were very important because they made use of large amounts of immigrant labour.

They eventually moved out into their own small homes, they tended to spread out and develop different Irish sections or Irish ghettos. The oldest one would have often been called 'The Patch' – that was true here of the earliest Irish

> *settlement in the Cabbotville section of Springfield which becomes Chicopee and also Holyoke. They tended to call it 'The Patch', I suppose, indicating it was pretty humble living conditions in which people live in...*[10]

The usual pattern of emigration from the Blaskets is evident in the story of Seán Tom Ó Cearnaigh. Seán was born on the island in 1882, and had seven brothers and sisters. He emigrated to Boston in the United States in 1901, and returned to the island in 1914 (an unusual fact in itself). Three of his brothers, Tomás, Muiris and Micheál, and one of his sisters, Nellie, also emigrated, which left only three on the island. One of those who stayed at home, Pádraig, had eight children; Éibhlís died from tuberculosis in infancy, and Céit, Máire, Eibhlín, Máiréad and Tomás emigrated. Only two remained in Ireland. After returning from America Seán Tom had ten children, one of whom, Seamus, died in infancy. Seven of the others emigrated to the Holyoke–Springfield area, which left only two, Seán and Céit, in their native island. Seán died tragically in 1947, aged only twenty-five years.[11]

There is a panel in the 'Emigration' section in the Great Blasket Centre's permanent exhibition which highlights, in green, those who stayed in their native area and, in purple, those who emigrated to America (see photographs in central plate section).

The plight of the Seán Tom Kearneys is also highlighted in the excellent book *Hungry for Home – Leaving the Blaskets*, penned by English author Cole Moreton.[12]

After World War Two, a number of young West Kerry people went to Great Britain, as there was plenty of employment there, especially as building labourers. But a lot more headed west, on the crest of the last emigration wave which resulted in the abandonment of *An Blascaod Mór*.

As well as that, in the decades before the final abandonment in 1953, some island families migrated to the mainland at Dún Chaoin and elsewhere in West Kerry. The author Peig Sayers and her son Mícheál, the poet, as well as her brother in law, migrated to the mainland in 1942. Eibhlís Ní Shúilleabháin was the wife of Seán Ó Criomhthain, son of Blasket author Tomás Ó Criomhthain. Eibhlís and Seán got married on the island and moved into Tomás's house, as he was, by then, an old man. It is evident from her letters to an English visitor to the island, Mr George Chambers[13], that Eibhlís was not at all happy with life on the island and that she wanted to leave. Some of her letters to Chambers were published in book form as *Letters from the Great Blasket*.

By early 1942[14] it is evident that Eibhlís and her husband Seán are quite determined to leave the island for good. At this stage, their only child, Niamh, is almost at school-going age. Thus she writes on 23 February 1942:

> *We have determined at last to leave this lovely Island, I know you will be very sad to hear it, but things are not as they should be and times are changed and especially for us here with a child at school age and no school and people saying and telling us the child must go to school very soon. They may take her away somewhere when they think of it you would know, so we thought it best to go out somewhere ourselves and try and have at least one joy out of this hard life, to live with our child. So the next time you will come to this Island there will be no Eibhlís but the ruins of the house, only the walls as we are taking out the head (roof) of the house there near Ballydavid as Seán's friends are living there with them. You may be sure I'll miss the calm air of our dear Island and the beautiful White Strand.*[15]

Eibhlís, Seán and Niamh left the island for good on 14 July 1942 and came to Muirríoch, on the mainland. In her account of 6 November 1942, we find Eibhlís and her husband residing on the mainland and she tells us that Peig Sayers and other family members have also re-settled on the mainland:

> *You may have heard that also our Queen Peig has come out (from the island) and is once more living in Dunquin in her native place; her brother-in-law was very very lonely but Mike (her son) was not, nor either Peig I heard. So pity our Island without either King or Queen this winter nor children on its ground, no wonder it's lonely and sad after all the gay families and all its children in foreign grounds. Remember (when) you once told me that Peig – the Queen – must be very happy there on the island, I told you there was nothing there in life to make her happy and like all Queens she had a bit of money too but far from being happy, nobody knows the worries and nervous that follows an islander's life.*[16]

One of the most remarkable island characters was Máire Uí Dhuinnshléibhe Ní Shé, or 'Méiní' as she was called. In his book *Méiní – The Blasket Nurse*[17], the author Leslie Matson tells us Méiní was born of Kerry parents in Chicopee Falls, Massachusetts, USA; how she came 'home' to West Kerry when she was a child; how she returned to the States in her teenage years; how she returned to Ireland again, and how she eloped to the Great Blasket Island to marry a widower quite a few years her senior.

Mr Matson has also compiled the biographies of some 120 islanders and this work, as yet unpublished, is called 'Blasket Lives' and is available in the library of the Great Blasket Centre.

Mr Matson describes how Méiní decided to leave the island:

> *At the beginning of March, 1932, after a spell of illness, Seán Eoghain died.*[18] *We are lucky to have a dated letter from Eilís Ní Shúilleabháin, the daughter-in-law of Tomás Ó Criomhthain, to her friend George Chambers, in which she describes the subsequent happenings.... As Eilís comments: 'to the sick man it brought peace and rest, to his poor wife, it has left her a lonely widow with her only comfort in life, her only son and daughter far far away from her'. Séamus*[19] *was at this stage in Canada, and Máire*[20] *in Springfield. Ominously, Eilís adds 'It is not her own house now'.*
>
> *Probably about six months later, before the equinoctial gales set in, Méiní said goodbye to her island home.*[21] *Seán Pheats Tom Ó Cearnaigh remembered bringing her across the Blasket sound with the postman, Seán Pheats Mhicí (whose father the King had died about three years before). In the postman's naomhóg she took a small amount of her property, including a mattress. Her mother was of course delighted to have her home again, for the old woman was now approaching her eighties and the physical strength for which she had been known (handling the bags of flour from Willie Long of Ballyferriter whose agent she was) was sadly on the wane. Seán and Méireas, the grandparents, were long since dead.*[22]

The main reasons for migrating from the island can be summarised as follows:

- Poverty, unemployment and isolation
- 'Subsistence' living; large families; substandard housing; inclement weather; long hard winters

- '*Is glas iad na cnoic i bhfad uainn*'… (Far away hills appear greener…)
- Some money made on mackerel fishing from around 1890 to 1921 facilitated passages to America
- A realisation that money could buy comforts and improve lives
- 'Gold on the streets' in America
- Everyone was leaving….

Because of emigration, almost all the indigenous families in West Kerry have lots of relatives in America and in Springfield, Massachusetts in particular. My own family is no exception. My father, Willie, RIP, who was the youngest in his family, had eight siblings, six of whom emigrated to the USA. They eventually got married and raised families there – so I have more cousins in the States than in Ireland. When I was a boy, the cities of Springfield and Hartford were more familiar to me than Cork or Limerick. My father told me that he never remembers seeing his eldest brother, Pádraig, who resided in Hartford, Connecticut. Such was the curse of emigration.

An uncle on my mother's side died in an incident on a New York street and, even to this day, I do not have much information about him. Another uncle spent most of his working life in Barry, Wales, but returned home on retirement.

My uncle Tom married Katherine Kearney, a Blasket lady, in Springfield and they raised a family there. He served for a while in the US army and subsequently in the armoury in Springfield.[23]

His daughter, my first cousin, Mrs Kathleen Arduini, had this to say in the documentary film *Blasket Roots – American Dreams*[24]:

My mother came to the States at 19 years old and I now have two sons that are 22 and 23[25] *and I can't imagine how difficult it was for someone to leave, not even a state but an entire country, and come across the ocean and of course in those days never knowing when they would be back again.*

My mother, she was a daughter of Peats Tom[26] *and he and my grandmother on her side, they were always so much part of the conversation and of her life and letters that did come back and forth, that they were in fact very, very real to me. How did anybody watch their children one after another go out in the boats and maybe never see them again. My mother was the first in her family to come to America and she came with a trunk and all her worldly possessions in it and then shortly after when she was able to provide a great part of the means for her sister Mary to come, then her sister came, then there was another sister Eibhlín and another sister Máiréad and a brother Tomás who also came out to this country and lived in the Springfield area so we were very close to them also.*

They would work in different homes in the capacity of cleaning and cooking.

When my father and mother got married they took a place on Case St. in Springfield. It was a great neighbourhood which is what they wanted for their children. They were there until I was born; after I was born they were able to buy a tenement in Hungry Hill[27] *on Silver St. I am the oldest and then I have 2 younger brothers. They wanted a place for us to be happy and be able to run around.*

Most of the West Kerry people actually achieved what they sought in the United States – a better life for themselves and their children. Most of them worked hard and held two jobs. A West Kerry community came into existence on Hungry Hill in Springfield and it is reputed that, a few generations ago, there was more Irish Gaelic than English spoken outside the Catholic Church in the area, Our Lady of Hope, on Sunday mornings. It is a sad fact of life that the same church and its community centre were closed down recently. The descendants of the West Kerry immigrants have moved out to the suburbs or to other cities and Puerto Ricans are taking their place.

While the West Kerry community was thriving on Hungry Hill and elsewhere, they never forgot their kith and kin at home. Dollars were sent home for Christmas in registered envelopes. Parcels of clothes were also sent home and I remember parcels coming to my own home in the late fifties and early sixties of the last century. It was an occasion for all the village when a parcel from America was received and all the neighbours would come in for the 'opening of the parcel'.

Mícheál Ó Cearna (Mike Carney – he spells his surname with a 'c' instead of the usual 'k') was born on the Great Blasket Island almost ninety years ago. He left the island at a young age and served in the bar trade in Dublin for a few years until he, also, emigrated to his relatives in Springfield. His brother, Seán, died of meningitis on the island in early 1947, while Mike was working in Dublin. His brother's death was the straw that broke the camel's back as far as the Great Blasket community was concerned. Consequently, Mike Carney contacted the Irish Government to do something about the plight of the islanders. The eventual outcome was the abandonment of the Great Blasket.

There are now fewer than ten Blasket islanders still alive. Three of them – including Mr Carney – still reside in Springfield – all from the extended Ó Cearna family. As the eldest living Blasket islander and as a representative of all the islanders – living and dead, including all the authors – Mr Carney was conferred with an honorary D. Litt. degree by the National University of Ireland, Maynooth, at a ceremony in the Great Blasket Centre in October 2009.

This paper concludes with an interview given by Mr Carney recently:

Was life on the Island happy or was it tough?

Well it was happy because we had to make it happy, the people made it happy but they had a tough life, they had, depending on fishing mostly, a little farming – the crux of the matter was the weather mostly in the wintertime. You never knew when you would get a storm.

Tell me about your brother Seán and how he died?

My brother Seán died in 1947. He got very sick before Christmas in 1946 … severe headaches and the weather was so bad that they could not go to the mainland to get a doctor or a priest or a nurse to help him and he died unfortunately on 5th January 1947.

A lot of people say, Maidhc, when your brother Seán died that was the end of the Island?

Well, I believe it was myself and the people of the Island too – I was in Dublin at the time. It was heart breaking – young fellow like that – twenty-four years of age and no way to help him, and if there was maybe he would be living today.

So the conclusion was that they had to move the Islanders off the Island?

Yes, after that I had left; my brother Maurice had left; the youth had to move and when you lose the youth you finally start losing the movements of the people on the Island – the young people. The old people had a tough time trying to manage.

And at about that time you and others started to try to persuade the Irish Government to move the remaining Islanders off the Island?

I had. I wrote to the Government … about the death of my brother … and I kept putting the pressure on them all the time to do something for the people whom I left on the Island before it was too late; and they finally listened to us, I guess after five years. It took that length of time.

And when did they finally move the Islanders off and how many Islanders were left?

There were about twenty altogether and they were all up in their sixties, eighties, seventies – my father was in his seventies when he went to the mainland and it was amazing what he said to Eamon deValera the Prime Minister of Ireland when he came to the Island[28] to talk to them. He said 'Sir, please get us somewhere where we can walk' and he moved to a place called Ballydavid … with my sister.

Good, tell us about your own journey Mike, when did you leave the Island?

I left the Island in 1937. There was nine of us in the family and I was the first to leave – ah I felt that somebody had to make a move … my father lost his wife at an early age – she was only thirty-seven years of age and it wasn't easy.… So I made up my mind that I would leave the house. We had five aunts and three uncles in Springfield. Incidentally we had more relatives in Springfield than we had in the Island.

And where did you go first?

…I went to Dublin and I served my apprenticeship to be a barman for three years. I spent eleven years working in Dublin as a Barman.…

And then when did you come to the United States?

In 1948, 5th May 1948, I sailed from Southampton in England on the *Queen Mary*. I was the first to arrive in New York from my family and then that particular time you had to have affidavits from your relatives in this country supporting your arrival to this country and they were responsible for you.

Why did you settle in Springfield Mass.?

That's where all my relatives were; my three uncles were here, five aunts and a couple of people from West Kerry had arrived before me. We always used to write to them and they used to send us gifts and even money for Christmas and stuff like that. Yea, Springfield was our second home.

What did you do for work in this country?

Well I didn't go bartending … I had enough of that in Dublin. I went to work in the supermarket place. I served my time with them. It wasn't easy because I wasn't ever in a supermarket in my life. And I went to night school to better myself. I took up a course in Business Administration – I had to pay for it myself too. There was no free tuition in them days in that category and it helped me along in the store and gave me a better idea how to do things and I finally ended up there as manager after a certain number of years. They were good to me – they were a good company in them days.

And after the A&P [Atlantic & Pacific Tea Company, a major supermarket chain]?

A&P Yes. I decided after twenty-five years with them, no, twenty-seven years, excuse me, that was enough and I got appointed as an officer of the Court House at the Hall of Justice – New Hall of Justice which was great and I spent twenty years there.

Tell us about some of your activities in Springfield to promote Irish culture.

I spent ten years teaching the Gaelic language – mostly adults they were, belonged to the Hibernians and they were born in this country of Irish descent and they were very dedicated people – the conversation was Gaelic, you know – meeting one another and they enjoyed it and I enjoyed it and believe it or not I got paid for it.

Tell us about Gaelic football in America.

We had quite a few of the young fellows from West Kerry came over here from Dunquin, Ballyferriter, Ventry, Dingle and I always thought that if we stayed together we'd be better for it you know. We started a Gaelic football team in 1949 and that particular year we won the New England Championship. I happened to be manager.

Tell me for how long were you involved in the John Boyle O'Reilly Club?

I spent sixteen years as an elected president, year after year, and during the sixteen years we accumulated $38,000 net profit which brought us to the purchase of the present building up in Progress Ave – 33 Progress Ave, a brand new building – there's nothing there only the four walls … a pain in the neck. Kept me thinking at night but we went through it and it's there today and the membership kept increasing every year. We went from fifty members in 1960 and I believe the club today, and the latest report I got, we've got a thousand members. It's a membership club.

Tell us a little about your efforts to preserve the Island back home and the Blasket Island Centre and then the National Park.

The Island evidently never left my system. They call me the old man of the Island now and I'm the only one left of that age. I thought the Island deserved better than being the way it was. I thought it deserved recognition for all the work it did on behalf of the Gaelic language and the Irish books and the people. They spoke the language and taught the language and the culture and the relationship. I thought the island deserved better fate than being left there with birds and rabbits and whatever else you've got and people going in to visit it. So I'm glad to hear finally that the Government has bought three-quarters of the property in the island now and eventually I hope – while I'm living – bring about the creation of an Historical Park and maybe create an area in there – some kind of museum form, not on a big scale, to show the visitors how the people used to live there, how they used to make their own clothes, how they used to make their own violins for music.

How they used to make their own canoes, the boats. You had to be very handy in the island and I wasn't one of them no, I never went in for carpet training, my brother Maurice did, he could do anything with his hands. How the people survived there, how they fished during the summer, lobster and crab fishing. Fished in the winter and how they talked and got along together. How they settled their own problems within themselves – there were no court house there….

Notes

1. S. J. Connolly (Editor), *Oxford Companion to Irish History*, Oxford University Press, 2004, p. 179.
2. The Great Famine or *An Gorta Mór* occurred between 1845 and 1848, when the potato crop was ravaged by blight or *Phytophthora infestans*.
3. Cecil Woodham-Smith, *The Great Hunger*, Hamish Hamilton Ltd., 1962.
4. Late 2009 – early 2010.
5. www.cso.ie
6. The western part of the Dingle Peninsula, County Kerry, Ireland.
7. Maurice O'Sullivan (Muiris Ó Súilleabháin), *Twenty Years A-Growing*, Oxford University Press, paperback, 1983, pp. 216–218.
8. Deeds registered in and around Springfield in the middle part of the nineteenth century contained family names very familiar on the Great Blasket and on the Dingle Peninsula, like the following: Sullivan, John 1847 Washington Street; Kane, John 1848 Wilcox Street; Dunlavy, Hugh & Dunlavy, Murty 1856 Wilcox Street; Carney, Margaret A. 1888 Bancroft & Chestnut Streets.
9. Maurice O'Sullivan (Muiris Ó Súilleabháin), *Twenty Years A-Growing*, *op. cit.*, pp. 235–236.

10. Professor Tom Moriarty in the documentary film *Blasket Roots/American Dreams*, commissioned by the Great Blasket Centre and shot in Springfield in 1997. Some 900 people came to view the premiere in Elms College on a very wintry night and all those in the audience claimed close West Kerry roots.
11. Information collected from the Blasket Genealogy in the Library of the Blasket Heritage Centre.
12. Cole Moreton, *Hungry for Home – Leaving the Blaskets*, Viking, 2000.
13. Some say that there was a romantic spark between Chambers and Ní Shúilleabháin.
14. Tomás Ó Criomhthain died on 7 March 1937.
15. Eibhlís Ní Shúilleabháin, *Letters From The Great Blasket*, The Mercier Press, 1992, p. 87.
16. Eibhlís Ní Shúilleabháin, *Letters From The Great Blasket*, *op. cit.*, p. 36.
17. Leslie Matson, *Méiní – The Blasket Nurse*, Mercier Press, 1995.
18. Méiní's husband.
19. Méiní's son.
20. Méiní's daughter.
21. Méiní was only forty-four years old at the time.
22. Leslie Matson, 'Blasket Lives', Great Blasket Centre Library.
23. Where they made the Springfield rifle.
24. Filmed in Springfield 1997.
25. One of her sons, a rookie policeman, died tragically in a road accident, two years after the film was made.
26. Peats Tom Ó Cearnaigh – as in the Kearney chart in the photograph.
27. Most of the West Kerry emigrants settled on Hungry Hill, Springfield, Massachusetts.
28. In July 1947 – a few months after Seán's death.

3

❧

Emigration from the Outer Hebrides – An Overview

Bill Lawson

Introduction

If no man is an island unto himself, as John Donne wrote, then no island community is self-contained either. To an islander, the sea is a highway, not a boundary, and it is little wonder that the routes from the Scottish islands of the north-west led west across the Atlantic, rather than east and south to the Scottish mainland, England and Europe. Even as late as the census of 1891, it is noticeable how few families there were from the Outer Hebrides living in the cities of Edinburgh and Glasgow, though there were of course many individual persons, working there and perhaps marrying there.

In the Visitor Centre at *Seallam!*, in Northton on the Isle of Harris, Northton Heritage Trust have built up a vast resource of information on all families who have been in the Outer Hebrides – from Lewis in the north to Barra in the south – in the last 250 years; and we are currently engaged on the last stages of a three-year project, partly funded by the Heritage Lottery Fund, tracing families who have emigrated from our islands – tracing families primarily, as to try to trace all the individuals, such as merchant seamen, who left would be a well-nigh impossible task.

So far, we have been able to identify more than 20,000 people who left the islands between 1750 and 1900. There are many more still to identify, and of course there are many hundreds who left so early and so informally that they can probably never be identified. In addition to identifying individual families, the scale of the project is allowing us to identify trends in the patterns of emigration from different islands at different times, and perhaps even more importantly to quantify the numbers of persons involved in each emigration.

At the time of the Emigration Conference, the *Seallam!* project contained information on 21,082 emigrants. This number is ever-increasing, as new sources of material are added to the project, but the main areas of emigration are now incorporated, and the final figure is unlikely to exceed 25,000. At the same time, the total figures may need to be reduced slightly, to allow for cases where, for example, young children died between the last date at which they appear in records here and the actual date of family emigration, but such adjustments will only have a minor effect on the final totals.

The figures to date for emigrants from the individual islands are as follows:

Barra	2,898
South Uist	5,774
North Uist	3,328
Harris	2,610
Lewis	4,657

The balance consists of families who are known to have emigrated from the Outer Hebrides, but whose original provenance has not yet been definitely ascertained. Immediately noticeable is the relatively small figure from Lewis, as this island was much more affected by internal migration than by overseas emigration.

Each island group had its own favoured area for emigration at different periods. Barra emigrants favoured Cape Breton, while South Uist tended more to Prince Edward Island and Cape Breton, and later to Ontario. North Uist emigrants settled in great numbers in Cape Breton, though in the 1850s many families went with the Highlands and Islands Emigration Society to Australia. Harris families also went to Cape Breton and Australia, while Lewis families went overwhelmingly to Quebec, and Ontario.

So let us look at these and other areas, in a chronological system, and see who went where, when and why.

Carolina

Few from the islands were involved in the transportations after the Jacobite rebellions of 1715 and 1745 – most of those involved seem to have been able to drift back home out of sight! – but the rebellions were in one sense the cause of the first great emigration from the Outer Hebrides to Carolina.

The tacksmen – holders of farms on long leases – in the islands had been mainly relatives of the clan chiefs, holding their lands because of their relationship to the chiefs, but in the new social system after Culloden they were expected to offer competitive money rents against sheep-farmers from the mainland. Rather than suffer the loss of prestige, and cash, many of them decided to go to Carolina with all their subtenants and work-force, with the aim of perpetuating the old social system there, with themselves as mini-chiefs. This was particularly so on Skye and the west coast, as noted by Johnson and Boswell on their tour; but Donald Campbell of Scalpay in Harris, Murdo MacLeod of Kilpheder in North Uist and Donald Morrison of Cross in Ness, Lewis were among the emigrant tacksmen, and of course Flora MacDonald and her husband.

They had hardly got there when the American War of Independence broke out. Most of the tacksmen had little love for the Hanoverian government at home in Britain, but they had even less love for republicanism, and so they fought on the British side, and lost. Some moved to Canada as United Empire Loyalists, and others, like Flora MacDonald, had to return to Scotland. Many of the subtenants and farm-workers took the republican side, and after the rout of Moore's Creek, even those who had supported the British found it politic to drift across the mountains into Tennessee and Georgia, and even to change their names into forms less obviously Highland.

Probably the number of settlers from the Outer Hebrides was never higher than in the hundreds, but tracing them now is well-nigh impossible, with the scarcity of records on both sides of the Atlantic.

New York

A much greater emigration, though less well-known today, was from Lewis to New York and Pennsylvania. In the year 1772–1773 alone, a British government report lists 831 emigrants to North America from the four Lewis parishes alone – and who knows how many there were in other years. One of the chief emigration agents was Daniel MacLeod, tacksman of Balallan and merchant in Stornoway, and brother of John MacLeod of Colbecks in Jamaica, who managed to persuade the Lord Lyon of the day that he was the true chief of the MacLeods of Lewis, on evidence almost as shaky as that which claims that the Australian descendants of MacLeod of Raasay are the true chiefs of the MacLeods of Lewis today – but this is not the occasion for straying into that minefield!

Many of those leaving Lewis were of merchant families, like Ready Money John MacIver and his nephew Alexander MacKenzie the explorer, or the MacIvers who co-founded the Cunard Shipping Line, and the landlords were worried about this loss of capital. Others left on vessels like the *Friendship of Philadelphia* in 1774, with 106 passengers from Lewis 'in order to procure a living abroad as they were quite destitute of bread at home', but Seaforth, the landowner, tried to prevent them in the courts from leaving, as he would be losing much of his work-force for labour-intensive industries such as kelp (seaweed).

After the American War of Independence it was probably not too politic to stress a Scottish ancestry, but it is clear that there are many families in New York and area who can claim ancestry from Lewis, even though details are not now remembered.

Hudson's Bay

In the late 1700s the Northwest Company and its trading rival the Hudson's Bay Company had done much of their recruiting in the Orkneys, but by the 1800s they both had shifted their main recruiting grounds to Lewis and Harris. Islanders were with the Companies at all levels, from Donald Ross who was Chief Factor at Norway House, to the many hundreds of trappers working in the northern wilderness – *an Talamh Fuar*, the Cold Country, to the Gael. Many of the Orkney men had married wives of the Cree Nation, and many of the Lewis men married their daughters and settled all over the Canadian North – while some of them brought wives and children home to Lewis, where there is a surprising amount of Cree Nation blood still. Others were like Peter MacLean from Leurbost, who fell out with the Company, but forgot the imperative rule – to get home first! – and ended as the progenitor of families in the wastes of central Labrador!

Many of the Company workers stayed on in Canada, but even more important in the story of emigration were the many who returned to the islands, bringing word of a new land and opportunities far better than could ever be available in the economically depressed and over-populated Islands.

Prince Edward Island

The 1770s were a time of religious repression in the islands of Barra and South Uist. These islands had always been Roman Catholic, but some of the landowners had changed to Protestantism, and expected their tenants to do the same. MacDonald of Boisdale in particular threatened to evict any tenants who did not change, and the Roman Catholic Church helped to arrange an emigration to Prince Edward Island (PEI), where MacDonald of Glenalladale on the Scottish mainland set up a Roman Catholic settlement around Scotchfort and Tracadie. Boisdale took fright at the prospect of losing so many of his work-force, and cancelled the evictions, but several South Uist families, together with others from Barra, joined the Tracadie settlement. Many others followed over the years, though they soon left the Glenalladale settlement to spread to settlements of their own, from Pierre Jacques on Lot 8 in the far west to Launching Point on Lot 55 in the east, while others moved on to the new settlements being formed in Cape Breton.

Because this emigration was so early, and PEI records are particularly poor and late in starting, it is very difficult to trace individual families. The first detailed census is not until 1871, by which time most of the original settlers had died, and we have to rely largely on newspaper obituaries and cemetery inscriptions, which at their best can only give a partial account of the community. The sheer number of MacDonalds who went to PEI over the years is another problem, and it is always a relief to meet a 'diagnostic' name such as Steele or O'Henley, which demonstrates beyond doubt a South Uist ancestry.

Nova Scotia

A few families settled on mainland Nova Scotia – some from the Roman Catholic islands of South Uist and Barra settled around Arisaig and Antigonish, while others from Lewis settled along the Gulf Shore from Wallace to Pugwash – which incidentally has had bilingual Gaelic and English road signs for more than fifty years!

Neither of these can be said to be a major island settlement, and both are extremely difficult to trace for the same reasons as those on PEI, with the main sources again being restricted to cemetery inscriptions and obituaries in newspapers such as the *Presbyterian Witness*, which by definition excluded those Roman Catholic families in the area. However, unexpected sources can still appear, as with the clients who arrived at *Seallam!* only a few weeks ago with a manuscript history of their family from the time of the original settlement in 1810.

Cape Breton

The great area for settlement from the islands in the first half of the nineteenth century was the island of Cape Breton – officially part of Nova Scotia, but very much a community in its own right. The first island settlers there seem to have been from Barra, from where soldiers had been at the Siege of Louisburg in 1758, and came back to Barra, not merely with reports of good land, but detailed instructions as to where would be the best land for settlement – on the shore of the Bras d'Or, an inland sea in the centre of the island – on either side of the Narrows now known as the Barra Strait.

New land was available on Cape Breton, and it was the first landfall in America for shipping crossing the Atlantic from the islands, so it is not surprising that it became the Promised Land for island emigrants.

At home, the kelp trade, burning seaweed for the minerals in its ash, had created an economic boom during the years of the French Revolutionary and Napoleonic wars, when supplies from elsewhere had been stopped by blockades and embargoes. Although the landlords of course made most of the profits, the crofters made enough to be able to save for their fare across the Atlantic and to acquire land in Cape Breton.

Each island had its own preferred area there, where new settlers would have the assistance of relatives and ex-neighbours – North Uist settlers gathered around the valley of the Mira River and between there and the shore at Catalone in Cape Breton County, with later settlements in the intervening hill country around Big Ridge and Trout Brook and the Bengal Road, with smaller settlement centres around Loch Lomond in Richmond County and at East Lake Ainslie in Inverness County.

South Uist families tended to gather around East Bay and Beaver Cove in Cape Breton County, with their religious centre at Boisdale, along the river valley of Grand Mira and at Mabou and West Lake Ainslie in Inverness County, among the major settlements in these areas from the Clanranald lands of the west coast of mainland Scotland.

There were smaller Lewis settlements at Little Narrows in Inverness County and St Anns in Victoria County, while Harris families were spread around Framboise and Grand River in Richmond County, and the North Shore of St Anns in Victoria County, with another group at the head of West Bay in Inverness County.

Barra settlers tended to stay around their original settlements at Iona and Christmas Island, on either side of the Barra Strait in Victoria and Cape Breton counties, but there were also sizeable communities on Boularderie Island in Cape Breton County and around Red Islands in Richmond County.

The kelp trade had been a wartime one, and after Waterloo in 1815 other supplies of minerals became available once more, and the kelp trade of the islands collapsed, taking the economy of the whole area with it. For a time some landlords offered rent reductions for the high levels set in the days of the kelp, as in North Uist in 1827, but crofters could no longer earn money to pay even the reduced rents, so the landlords began the period of clearance to create sheep-farms. Harris, the Uists and Barra suffered particularly badly from the Clearances, with whole areas of the islands cleared of their people, who were at first sent to Cape Breton. There, most of the good land had been taken up already, and the later settlers had to make do with the backlands and high valleys, where the soil was poor and the winter came early and stayed late. Most had no capital coming, and little chance of earning any from poor land, and great numbers of the later settlers ended up working in the coal and iron mines of Sydney and Glace Bay.

Cape Breton is the first area in which there is a reasonable chance of identifying both where emigrants came from and also where they settled. So far in our project we have traced more than 5,000 emigrants to Cape Breton from the Outer Hebrides – 533 from Barra, 1,238 from South Uist, 1,200 from North Uist, 582 from Harris and 210 from Lewis. The figures do not add up, because there are others whose source has still to be identified, and the final figures will be considerably higher, as there are some areas still to be completely surveyed.

Quebec

In the 1840s the west of Scotland, like Ireland, was visited by potato blight, and if famine on the Irish scale was averted here, it was mainly due to the efforts of voluntary bodies, especially the churches, with government help and assistance, at least at first, from several landlords. Potato blight was in Cape Breton too, so there was no longer any sense in going there, so emigration moved into Canada proper – Lower Canada, now Quebec, and Upper Canada, now Ontario.

Emigration from Lewis to Quebec commenced in 1838, when twenty-four families settled in what were to become Lingwick and Bury Townships in the *Cantons de l'Est*, or Eastern Townships of Quebec. The Eastern Townships are in the south-east of Quebec, near the borders with New Hampshire and Maine in the United States. There had already been English settlements to the west, around the city of Sherbrooke, and French settlements to the north, in the wide plains of the shores of the St Lawrence, but Bury and the lands east to the US boundary were high hill-lands, heavily forested, around the central massif of Mont Megantic (3,600ft), empty, and ready for settlement.

The original plan was for the emigrants to seek work on the farms around Melbourne, in the fertile valley of the St Francis River, where farmers like Colin MacIver, formerly tacksman of Gress in Lewis, had settled, but the lure of land of their own was too great for most of the emigrants, and twenty-four families moved on to land offered for sale by the British-American Land Company. There had been a small settlement around Victoria prior to the Lewis settlement, but the land there was poor, and the settlers had abandoned their cabins and headed for the western gold-rush. The Lewis settlers, mainly along what is still known as the Scotch Road in Bury, had better land and were able to survive the first winter by supplying timber ash in return for credit from the British-American Land Company. There was plenty of timber for building cabins, and it is said that the shortage of nails etc. was solved by some settlers by burning down cabins in Victoria and salvaging the nails from the ashes!

Word of the opportunities in the Eastern Townships must have gone back to Lewis quickly, for in 1841 a further thirty families arrived. We can be more precise about the origins of families in this case, as the Quebec census, though nominally in 1841, was not in fact carried out till the following spring. Even though the Quebec census shows heads of households only, we can still trace almost all of the emigrants before they leave in the Scottish census of 1841, and after their arrival in the Quebec census of 1842.

The 1842 census shows a total of 260 Lewis settlers in the area, which by this time had spread up the Scotch Road through Lingwick and the side roads of North Hill, Fisher

Hill and Red Mountain towards Winslow Township. To this number will require to be added an unknown number of single children of settlers, helping out the family finances by working in established farms in the area or in the nearby city of Sherbrooke.

By 1851 there were more than 1,000 settlers of Lewis descent in the area, mainly around Gould and Lingwick and in the new town of Stornoway, PQ. By 1881 numbers had grown to almost 3,000 and the settlement area had spread to the east through Baile Shiadair and Baile Bharabhais to Springhill, Milan and Druim a' Bhaic and Balallan, to reach Lac Megantic itself, which gave its name to the famous Megantic Outlaw. He was Donald Morrison, of Uig, Lewis, ancestry, who had fallen out with a money-lender, also from Lewis, had killed a bounty-hunter who tried to arrest him, and had lived for a time hidden by his Lewis compatriots before finally being caught by the law.

By 1881 the total figure for the whole area was 2,872, which was probably the highest census figure, though even this figure would be understated by the numbers of family members working away from home at the time of the census. By 1891 the total had dropped slightly to 2,779, and by 1901 to 2,614. By this time the figures for all townships were falling, especially in Winslow, where the abandonment of the Middle District of Baile Shiadair and Baile Bharabhais had already begun.

There was always more land available for settlement in the Eastern Townships, and emigrants continued to arrive, even up to the 1920s, but the flood had by now diminished to a trickle. In the nature of things, the land available later was of poorer quality, and the families who settled there were among the first to move on.

Although much of the land in the Lewis settlement had good lumber for selling, and good leaf-mould in the ground, once this was exhausted, the land itself was generally rocky and poor, and many of the families there moved on farther west as the Prairies were opened up. Now much of the better land has been taken over by French-speaking settlers, and the poorer land has reverted to forest, and the last Gaelic-speaker in the rural area died a few years ago. But the Quebec settlement had given the Hebridean emigrants the chance to pull themselves out of their poverty, and to establish a foothold on the ladder to economic prosperity, elsewhere in the New World.

The settlement in the Eastern Townships was primarily a Lewis settlement, where we have traced 1,698 emigrants from Lewis so far; there were also small numbers there from Harris (64) and North Uist (36).

Australia

At the peak of the potato blight in the late 1840s, destitution was widespread through the islands. Any capital had long since been expended on buying food, and emigration was impossible without assistance with the fares. The Highlands and Islands Emigration Society (HIES) was set up with government assistance to encourage emigrants to Australia, which at that time was looking for steady family emigrants – who in theory at least would be less likely to head off to the gold-rush!

In the Outer Hebrides, the Society's efforts were concentrated on Harris and North Uist, from where emigrants sailed mainly on the ships *Priscilla*, *Hercules*, *Persian* and *Royal Albert*. We have traced 259 emigrants from North Uist and 455 from Harris, almost 10 per cent of the population of the latter island.

Among the emigrants on the *Priscilla* was a group from the island of St Kilda, but most of them died on the ship or in quarantine – from measles, to which they had never been exposed in their remote home, and to which they had no resistance.

The emigrants were not settled together but dispersed to where work was available – in theory in order to pay back a percentage of their fares – so there is no island settlement area in Australia to match that in the Eastern Townships of Quebec. In 1857 the HIES was wound up, and without their assistance would-be emigrants could not afford the fare to Australia. We have few details of families going after that date, until much more recent times.

Ontario

While the HIES was arranging emigration to Australia, the landlords of Lewis and South Uist and Barra preferred to make their own arrangements.

Sir James Matheson of Lewis had spent a fortune on poor relief in the worst days of the famine, but the problem was beyond what could be solved with even his resources. The poorest of the population were most in need of help, and emigration was beyond their reach, so he arranged free passage to Canada to all who would accept his terms. Since the alternative was cessation of all poor relief, they did not have much choice! Others were keen to emigrate given the chance, and Matheson arranged that those who wished could join their compatriots in the Eastern Townships of Quebec, and others would be taken to where new land was available, in Bruce County, Ontario, around the present town of Ripley.

Sir John Cathcart of South Uist and Barra was more concerned just to get rid of the superfluous population. He also provided free transport across the Atlantic, but that was all, and the emigrants were left starving and penniless on the quays of the St Lawrence. The Upper Canada Government had to take responsibility for them and find them land, most in Middlesex County, west of London, Ontario.

The Middlesex County settlement was centred around what is now the Church of St Columba, Bornish, whose graveyard contains many stones with diagnostic South Uist names such as O' Henley and Steele as well as innumerable MacDonalds, MacEachans and MacIntyres, among others. Some went to Glenelg Township in Grey County, south of Owen Sound, and others were scattered around Ontario wherever land was available at the time when they were fit and able to travel there. Some of the Middlesex settlers later made their way across Lake Huron to the Saginaw area of Michigan in the USA.

Altogether we have been able to identify 998 emigrants from South Uist and Benbecula to Middlesex County, 262 to Grey County, and another 400 scattered around, but mainly in the area around Stratford. The total for South Uist and Benbecula emigrants is currently 1,708, with a further 162 from Barra, most in Brant County.

Lord MacDonald of North Uist also sent out emigrants at this time, again mainly to Middlesex County, Ontario, but most of the emigration from his estates at this time was to Australia with the HIES.

In 1863 a further group of emigrants from Lewis settled around Goderich, on the shore of Lake Huron, and there was also a settlement from Harris, sponsored by Lady Dunmore, the proprietrix, around Collingwood, on the lands behind the shores of Georgian Bay.

Unlike the Quebec settlement, to which emigrants were still going in the 1900s, the Ontario settlements tended to be one-off settlements, on good land, which was soon all taken up. The only lands left available were on the Indian Reservations, such as the Bruce Peninsula, and many of the later settlements were on land taken from the Reservations as these were gradually diminished to make room for the new settlers.

So far we have located 3,746 emigrants to Ontario – including 1,870 from South Uist and Barra, 382 from North Uist, 319 from Harris and 1,089 from Lewis – but these are mainly to the rural areas, and there will be many more families who found work in the cities and never moved to the settlement areas.

Prairies

As the Canadian railroads spread west, lands for settlement became available along their tracks, with the added inducement of employment on track-laying to boost the income of the initial years. Many families went west from the established settlements in Quebec and Ontario, but there were also several sponsored schemes of emigration from the Outer Hebrides to the prairies.

Lady Gordon-Cathcart, owner of South Uist and Barra, sponsored an emigration to Wapella in Saskatchewan in 1883 and 1884, while the UK and Canadian governments combined in a Croft Colonization Scheme at Killarney in Manitoba and Saltcoats in Saskatchewan.

So far we have traced 881 emigrants on such schemes to the prairies – including 309 from South Uist, 213 from Harris and 273 from Lewis.

As late as the 1920s the Roman Catholic Church was sponsoring settlements at Clandonald and Vermilion in Alberta, and there was also a major move from North Uist to Vancouver, also in the 1920s, but we have not gathered statistics for these emigrations yet.

South America

Since then there have been emigrations from Lewis and Harris to South America, Lewis families going mainly to Patagonia and Harris families to the Falkland Islands, to work on the sheep-ranches, in surroundings and a climate with which the island people were well-qualified to cope. Many returned home after a tour of duty, and there is an area on the Isle of Scalpay, Harris, known as Falkland Terrace, because so many of the houses there were built by families returning from the Falklands. Other families remained in South America, where there are still Spanish-speaking MacLeods and MacIvers!

Concluding Remarks

The Outer Hebrides are beautiful, but life here was never easy – it still isn't! – and emigration is a necessity for far too many of its people, especially today. Their people have left their mark all over the world, to a degree far greater than the numbers of their population would suggest. It does not matter where you go in the world, you will meet someone from the Outer Hebrides.

After many years of historical denial of the Clearances, the pendulum now seems to have swung too far the other way, and emigration is all too often equated with clearance, with every emigrant from the Outer Hebrides driven unwillingly from home by a rapacious landlord. Clearances did happen, often under atrocious circumstances, but they are only a part of the story, and emigration was part of life in these islands long before the Clearances and long afterwards.

If we treat all emigrants as dispirited refugees then we have to explain what happened to them halfway across the Atlantic, for that is not how they arrived in the New World, where they took a new environment by the metaphorical scruff of its neck and made a new life for themselves there.

Of course there were some failures also – there are bound to be in any group of people – but perhaps we tend to dwell too exclusively on them. By concentrating on hardship and failure we demean the pioneers who left these islands to settle in new lands – and what message are we giving to the young people of today, if we tell them that their ancestors were helpless, hapless and hopeless, to quote a phrase I have heard used.

There is much to lament in the story of emigration, but surely there is much to be proud of also.

What we are trying to achieve in the emigration project at *Seallam!*, and what I have been trying to set out in this address, is to provide a time-frame and a relative scale of magnitude for different episodes of emigration, to give a wider perspective within which the history of emigration from the Outer Hebrides can be judged.

4

ଓ

Emigration to the Mainland – Songs and Recordings

Morag MacLeod

Robin Hall used to present a programme of folksongs on radio and I heard him say once that he didn't know if the Gaels had a word for homesickness. As one who was over there and saw (*tè a bha thall 's a chunnaic*) I took the chance shortly afterwards to tell Archie Fisher that the Gaels had invented 'homesickness' and he hasn't forgotten what I said. We owe a lot of our best songs to homesickness, and we should be grateful to our bards for putting our thoughts on love of people and place into an artistic form.

Homesickness was due to the movement of people between two very different environments, whether from choice or from necessity. I'm not going to go into the history of those movements, with experts in the audience into whose sailing wake I could never venture (reversing the usual translating of an English saying into Gaelic, *Feadhainn nach deidhinn a dh'uisge na stiùrach aca*). The subject I agreed on is emigration to the mainland, but in passing I want to mention movement between islands and within islands.

We can go back a long way. Among the waulking songs, many of which were supposed to have been composed before the seventeenth century, and which tradition-bearers from Barra and Uist have preserved for us, this one expresses feelings of nostalgia for life in another place:

'S fada 's is cian a chì mi sealladh uam
Chì mi Rùm is Eige 's Canaigh uam;
Gu tà chan fhaic mi na Hearadh uam
Far a robh mi òg nam leanabh
Mùirneach, meadhrach, gu ciùin arralach.

And again:

Siùbhlaidh mi 's fàgaidh mi 'm fearann
Falbhaidh mi air bòrdaibh daraich
Ruigidh mi tìr-mòr na Hearadh
Far an d'fhuair mi gu h-òg m'aran.

And of course there is that splendid song by Mary MacLeod when she was allowed back to Dunvegan, from we are not sure where (recording of William Matheson from *Theid mi lem dheòin*).

Which place becomes the object of the poet's art depends on circumstances. Present inhabitants of Scalpay might have been surprised that anyone with the intelligence to be a poet would wish to live anywhere else, but you can also imagine what a shock it was for people from the beautiful machair land of Pabbay to find themselves in such a muddy rocky place. A song to the tune of *Tha mi sgìth 'n fhògair seo* has a couplet,

Tha mi sgìth ann an Scalpaigh, eilean rapach nan seòltairean.

I came across another one rather disparaging of Scalpay recently. It goes:

Cha b'e am bothan crùbach
'S an ceap na bhalla-cùil ris
A chleachd mi na mo dhùthaich
'S an eilean chùbhraidh ghaincheadh.

Far robh na taighean àlainn
Chan ionnan 's mar a tha mi
An innear fo mo shàilean
'S am fàileadh ga mo mharbhadh.

It's interesting to learn that the Pabaich had progressed from the thatched cottage shared with the cows as early as the 1840s.

Moving from the east to the west side of Harris would ordinarily be regarded as a step up in the world, but the Cluer bard, Alasdair Ferguson, didn't think so when some of the inhabitants of the Bays were moved to the machair on the west coast. He states baldly, I would like to go to that place where my grandfather lived, at the Iodhlainn Mhòr. But no, he says,

De 'm math sin, cha teid mi ann,
Tha mo cheann air fàs bàn;
Gus an tèid mi chist' nam bòrd
Cha bhi m'fhearann mòr measg chàich.

(Sung by Catriona MacLeod, Geocrab).

We can surmise that the most likely reason for moving from one place to another would be to improve material circumstances. When the Statutes of Iona ordered that the oldest sons of clan chiefs had to go south for their education, and had to become fluent in English, it did not take the gentry long to accept Lowland ways and English language as superior. The picture is made very clear to us in Roderick Morison, *An Clàrsair Dall*'s poem to MacLeod of Dunvegan, the son of Iain Breac. Duncan Ban Macintyre, who moved to Edinburgh in the 1760s, seems to have been seduced by English. He says to the woman he loved, Màiri NicNeachdain,

> *'S ann thèid thu Dhun Eideann*
> *A dh'ionnsachadh Beurla.*

That attitude still holds in many places and with many people, that social and material improvement involves fluency in English.

Marriage, of course, would be considered as a means to improving one's social and material status. This song tells how a lady of high degree was deceived by a con man who promised her a castle and lands. When she married him she found out that those were all non-existent:

> *Gheall thu dhomh taigh mòr is sabhal san tadhaileadh na ceudan*
> *'S thuirt thu go robh agad buailtean 's buachaillean da rèir sin*
>
> *Cha robh taigh mòr agad no sabhal, ged a chuirinn feum orr'*
> *Ach bothan beag am bun a' bhruthaich bh'aig mo phiuthar-chèile.*

(Recording of song *Dh'fhalbh mi leis na lùban laghach*).

Songs on the theme of emigration began to emerge to a significant extent in the nineteenth century, when sheep-farming led to evictions, and industry attracted labourers from the Gaelic-speaking areas to Lowland cities. Poets like Neil MacLeod of Skye, John MacFadyen of Mull, John MacLachlan of Rahoy and Evan MacColl of Lochfyneside were all influenced by the Lowlands. Because their songs were published, they became popular amongst Highlanders who may well not have known who the authors of the songs were. Groups were formed in Glasgow, Edinburgh and London to bring together exiles from various islands, and it became possible for islanders to meet to indulge sentimentally in former customs. This included Gaelic church congregations as well as territorial associations. Poets thus got their audience and their most successful theme was liable to be nostalgia. Nostalgia was possibly a device on which to hang the wish to display one's poetic skills. In spite of the popularity of his songs about Skye, it is thought generally that Neil MacLeod enjoyed his cushy life in Edinburgh as a tea merchant, and that his salutes to and laments for his native land were not all that sincere. *Duanag a' Chìobair*, by Domhnall Phàil from Badenoch, must have been known to him, as he uses its metre for one of his songs of nostalgia:

Ged tha mise 'n Dun Eideann
Ann an comunn luchd Beurla
Chan eil m' inntinn ag èirigh ri 'n dòigh.

'S ann tha m' aigne 's mo dhùrachd
Ann an eilean nan stùchbheann
Far an eistinn ri crùnluath an eòin.

No doubt, however, he composed more songs of that genre than he would have if he had stayed in Skye. His repertory was different from that of his father, Donald, whose poems were more local and Clan MacLeod-based and his brother John, who was away from home, but as a sailor, composed more local poems.

I don't know if it's because of publications like *Bardachd Leòdhais* and especially *Eilean Fraoich* that we are so aware of songs of homesickness composed by Lewismen – very few by women. Choosing from the vast amount of material is easier because I have to confine myself to recordings that I happen to have. I have played this example to several Lewis audiences but have not yet found out who composed it. Its sentiment is fairly straightforward, the last stanza particularly so, leading one to be convinced of its sincerity: Some people like living in Glasgow, but I would prefer Lewis of the high hills (*Eilean Leòdhais mo ghaoil*).

The poets themselves sometimes counter the accusation of insincerity. Robert MacLeod from Na Geàrrannan in Carloway puts the question himself:

Ma thug thu do chridhe dha uile gu lèir,
Carson a rèist a dh' fhàg thu e?

And answers it:

Cha b'urrainn an dachaigh ar cumail le chèil
'S e 'n gille bu shine bu dlighiche greim.

Corstaidh MacDonald, Corstaidh Freadaidh, from Amhuinnsuidhe and Ceann Tùlabhaig, South Harris, declares at the start of her song that the only reason for leaving Harris for the mainland was to earn a living:

Na Hearadh àlainn far 'n deach ar n-àrach
Gum b'fheudar fhàgail air sgàth ar beòshlaint.

The Rev. Murdo Smith in Fagail Steornabhaigh doesn't give an answer to his own question:

> *Carson nach gabhainn còmhnaidh far 'n a thogadh òg mi suas*
> *Oir cha bhi dìth mo loin orm an Leòdhas nam beann fuar?*
> *Tha bradan agus fiadh ann, tha iasg gu pailt sa chuan*
> *'S tha fearann beairteach bòidheach a chinneas pòr le luach.*

(Jenna Cumming sings it beautifully).

Donald Macintyre from South Uist, settled in Paisley, has his own repertory of sad songs of homesickness. (Seumas Campbell recorded *Bun an Ròdh'* on a CD of Uist songs, *An Lorg nam Bàrd*).

But songs about life on the mainland were not always solemn. Mary MacPherson celebrated a game of shinty in Glasgow; Ruairi Mackay composed a popular song about the Uist and Barra Association. We cannot refer to Màiri or Ruairi MacAidh as emigrants, strictly, but their songs give a strong feeling of Highland Glasgow (Margaret Callan's rendition of the celebration of *Comunn Uibhist is Bharraigh* is on the same CD as Seumas Campbell's *An Lorg nam Bàrd*).

One of the earliest of the poets who did settle in Glasgow was John MacFadyen of Mull who lived from 1850 to 1935. In his books *Sgeulaiche nan Caol* and *An t-Eileanach*, he gives his own provenance as Glasgow. His song about the Irish in the Saltmarket fits a stereotype which one hopes is no longer accepted in Scotland, but I'm not so sure. Here is a verse or two:

> *Nuair chruinnich iad còmhla san taigh-òst aig Mackenna,*
> *'S ann ann a bha bhòilich mun dòigh bh'aig an seanair,*
> *Mar bhuaileadh e dhòrn is mar dh'òladh e searrag,*
> *'S ann bha e san t-sabaid ro threun.*

Then he lists a lot of Irish names:

Bha Bridget air cabhsair 's i dannsa ri Brolligan,
Ceann-ruisgte, cas-ruisgte, 's chnagadh i corragan,
Spreadadh i 'm poll a-nall mu na h-oiseanan
'S ghlaodh i le sodan "Ho-rè".

The names Michael Maginty, O'Rork, M'Gork, O'Branigan, Kelly, Flannigan, O'Rafferty and M'Cafferty as well as Ulster, Munster, Antrim, Leitrim, Connaught, Tralee, Limerick and Kildare are lovingly used by the poet for the purpose of his rhyme.

Donald Macintyre has a rich repertory of humorous songs which depict the atmosphere of Glasgow – or Paisley really – so admirably. In one song he looks back sorrowfully at the good times he had with his money when he was single. Now that he's married, he's working hard, but his wife uses it all up.

Chan fhàgar bùth an Glasachu gun siubhal ag iarraidh adaichean;
Bidh mise ruith nam Barachan mu'm faigh mi bloighean bhrògan
Tha sporan Dhòmhnaill 's e cho gann.

And he gives a vivid picture of how she goes home to Uist for the summer holidays while he stays at his job, and if he goes astray in *Bùth Dho'ill icLeòid* someone's bound to tell her. The closeness of the community is so apparent in such descriptions.

His picture of the pub he calls Donald MacLeod's Shop reveals one of the attractions for him of his home in the city, but he also displays his wonderful humour in a more national account of the taking of the Stone of Destiny. His translation of Burns' *Tam O' Shanter* is also independent of Uist or Paisley, but not of his strong, poetic Gaelic background.

Domhnall Ruadh doesn't make a great deal of use of English in his poems. Those who are most guilty of that are those who served in the Navy. My example, however, is from a soldier, *Cha mhol mi-fhin an t-saighdearachd* (the singer is Murdo Gillies from Bragar in Lewis).

The use of English and Gaelic together became a deliberate fashion for a time. My theory is that when they first came into close contact with English speakers, and especially technical terms such as were used in the services, bards were fascinated with it. The best-known begins 'When I came down to Glasgow first *a mach gu tìr nan Gall*'.

Emigrants to such as Glasgow, where large numbers from the same islands gathered, came to be quite at home after a while. The island men had their own ideas of Glasgow girls – very different, one is persuaded, from the nice girls at home. Murdo MacKenzie from Ness in Lewis doesn't even give his own wife the benefit of the doubt (the singer is Murdo John MacKenzie from Ness, and I am grateful to Radio nan Gaidheal for this song and the next one).

Bidh 'm pocair man a' chlagann ort

Many Gaels in Glasgow are ignorant of lots of things. They think they'll be well-off being married to a Lowlander, slim, shiny eyebrows, their nails peeping out from their shoes, but the poker will hit their skull as sure as they're there.

When they go in front of the minister, they are all misty, in their dress down to their ankles; a ring will be put on their finger. She'll start to laugh and she'll give him a kiss, but the poker...

When the reception is prepared and they sit at the table, there's her flowers on her chest and a cigarette in her hand. Whisky in the glasses, she can't wait to drink it and the poker…

When the wedding's over she'll take off to the pub, a shawl around her shoulders, an infant wrapped up. You thought, my lad, that you were in seventh heaven, but the poker…

Man, you're stupid if you don't avoid that type whom you see in the close-mouth holding fish and chips. Nails like eagles and a crooked nose, because the poker…

My own wee wifie, although she doesn't drink, her tongue is as nimble as a loom weaving cloth. She'll shout in such a temper, "Shut up! Keep quiet or you'll get the poker by the skull as sure as you're there".

And another fault is that they become uppity and will not look at the lads from home. The only reason that Murdo MacDonald from Borve, Lewis has no success with them, although he feels he should as a fellow-stranger in a strange land, is that they have become uppity since coming to Glasgow (performed by The Lochies).

Clann-nighean mo bhaile

The girls from my village who live in Glasgow, when I go past them I'm not worth a look. The girls from my village won't come near me.

When I go to the Bridge (a meeting place for Gaels in Glasgow, referred to as The Highlandman's Umbrella) on a Saturday evening, my companions are strangers, no-one else will have me.

They are not interested in sailors, navvies or builders. You're no use if you're not a policeman.

They have a bag on their arm with a mirror and comb, and their pockets smell of powder and rouge.

Some wear a fox fur around their necks, and bright spectacles from Woolworths on the nose.

With one of them to windward you'll be like a miller, with waves of powder falling off their nose.

5

☙

Quebec and the Eastern Townships of Canada: Emigration from the Outer Hebrides in the Nineteenth Century

Margaret Bennett

The vast area of Quebec situated on the Canadian border adjacent to the US states of Vermont and New Hampshire was once known as 'Lower Canada'. In 1834 a group of Montreal and London businessmen, 'The British-American Land Company', purchased around six million acres of the area known as the Eastern Townships (*les Cantons de l'Est*) intending to sell off farms to English-speaking immigrants. The land was divided into eight counties, three of which,[1] being rich and fertile, were bought up by affluent English and Lowland Scots farmers. The rest proved so useless for speculation that within a few years the Company was in severe debt, so, to cancel it, half a million acres reverted to the Crown. The Canadian Government, meanwhile, had begun a land-settlement scheme offering fifty-acre land grants to any British male subject willing to settle in Lower Canada.[2] Before long, British Government agents co-operating with this policy looked upon this swampy wilderness as a possible solution to Britain's Potato Famine crisis – it would be offered to famine victims as an incentive to emigrate.

The Scotsman of September 11, 1851 reported that Sir John Trevelyan, the Government official in charge of the emigration scheme announced that:

> *Ethnologically the Celtic race is an inferior one, and, attempt to disguise it as we may, there is naturally no getting rid of the fact that it is destined to give way to the higher capabilities of the Anglo-Saxons ... emigration to America is the only available remedy for the miseries of the race...*

The *Fifeshire Journal*, 1852, noted that Trevelyan 'contemplated with satisfaction ... the prospects of flights of Germans settling here [in Britain] in increasing numbers – an orderly, moral, industrious and frugal people, less foreign to us than the Irish or Scottish Celt...'.

Even before these shocking reports, however, emigration agents had been at work with estate factors (such as J. Munro MacKenzie in Lewis), identifying families to be cleared. Without exception they were Gaelic speakers, the majority monoglot, with neither the means nor the ability to read the newspaper reports of the day. The work of genealogist Bill Lawson and his wife Chris leaves no doubt as to the extent of the clearance, crofting township after township, family after family identifying connections to 'distant cousins' or kin in Quebec. A visit to any *Comann Eachdraidh* (Local Historical Society) collection and archive in Lewis, Harris and Uist reveals the raw memories stored in a huge range of items, from poignant letters to photographs of derelict houses, each one with an emotional as well as historical tie to Quebec. Despite the passing of time – more than a century and a half – there is still a sense of loss that is deeply moving. While immediate relatives grieved to see the emigrants depart, succeeding generations hold on to their memories and some still wonder what it must have been like to have been part of the uprooting.

This paper records the actual words of the descendants of emigrants, told through each generation and interpreted by the tellers themselves, all second, third and fourth generation Quebecois who have lived their entire lives in the Eastern Townships. The historian searching for comment upon political or social issues that affected emigration during the time of the Potato Famine will be disappointed. Among those who actually went through the experience, personal accounts of emigration usually begin on the ship: six or eight weeks of cramped conditions, storms, seasickness, cholera and, for some, death and bereavement. Their descendants still speak of the shock of landing in thick forest, encountering temperatures ranging from 30 degrees below in winter to searing, humid heat in summer, blackflies, mosquitoes, bears. To a people who had never known trees, far less swung an axe, such memories were enough to replace any famine story with ones about their first winter and the struggle to make a living.

The immigrants named their towns and villages after the ones they left – Stornoway, Tolsta, Dell, Gisla, Balallan, Ness, Back. They built churches and schools throughout the area, though, as in Gaelic Scotland, the schools came under an education policy that insisted on English as the *only* language of the classroom and playground. Their church services, however, were primarily Gaelic and they lined out the psalms as they had done back home – 'And we had good precentors in those days'. Daily family worship was also in Gaelic, and for some families remained so until the late 1970s.

The Gaels got on well with their French neighbours who, in the early days, were by far the minority. People were willing to lend a hand, no matter the language used to communicate. In 1992, eighty-one-year-old Russell MacIver, whose people came from Balallan, recalled with pride the skill of the carpentry in those days, as he described a 'barn-raising bee':

> *I saw one – I was pretty young … my uncle Neil MacDonald, he put one up in Balallan here. They had a bee to put the barn up… [Did he get help?] Gosh, the whole neighbourhood, maybe twenty, thirty men came … everything was all ready and fitted … just put it up and into place. And the ones that made those fittings, they knew what they were doing! They were all ready to put the wooden pin in – there were no nails then. And I remember one year there was a French fellow … and he came around one day and he asked my father 'You come tomorrow, help lift big barn?' [Laughs] Oh, about a mile further on… Oh yeah, everybody would help.*[3]

The pioneer settlers shared skills and learned new ones, some attaining legendary expertise, as in the use of the broad-axe or the pit-saw. The magnificent covered bridge near Gould, for example, was hand-sawn and constructed by such men. The French welcomed the expertise of experienced wheelwrights and millers who had learned their trade 'at home in Lewis'. Historian Donald MacDonald noted that a mill-stone was even sent from Lewis to Megantic[4] and to this day, old water-mills in Lewis testify to the technical skill attained in previous centuries.[5] In Stornoway, Quebec, a local oral history project records that in 1853 a French family, *les Legendres*, moved into the area to start a milling business: *'Les frères Legendre font construire le premier moulin à scie par Donald McLeod qui construisit plusieurs moulins dans la region'*.[6]

The grist-mill served a wide area and, as Russell recalled, a trip to the Legendre's Mill in Stornoway was an enjoyable day out as well as a necessary preparation for winter: 'And those old Legendres, they could talk Gaelic just as good as anybody else. And the second generation and the third generation they could talk a little'.

One of the skills the Gaels learned from their French neighbours was the use of the ingenious 'stump-puller' used in land clearing[7] though completely unknown to crofters who had once tilled peaty or sandy soil. For almost every aspect of life, there were huge adjustments to be made, not only to the extremes of temperatures but also to the landscape and vegetation, a combination of swampy wetland with thick brush and dense areas of conifers that had to be burned to create fields. Building materials and techniques contrasted hugely to those they had left behind, yet they soon learned how to make warm, comfortable homes and how to keep the kitchen cool in summer. There were maple groves with glorious autumn colour and springtime sap to be used for syrup-making, though, as Duncan McLeod wryly remarked, it was not quite as they had imagined when emigration agents told them they would 'only need to tap a tree' to get sugar. Homesteading proved to be endless hard work, yet with little opportunity to earn any money to buy farm implements necessary for improvement. Russell explained how they found a solution:

> *When it was haying time in Vermont, they'd walk from here up to Vermont to do the hay, and it was all that crooked sticks, you know. They didn't have mowing machines then ... just a scythe... And one time there was a bunch of men went up to Vermont, my great-uncle, Neil Beaton... They used to have to walk up there and walk back... My father*

> *had a cousin went up one time by bicycle, then came back... Well, the time that Dave Nicolson's grandfather went, he died there – they were in the haying, that'd be July probably. And his wife didn't hear about his death until they walked back in September or October... It was one hot day, oh, it was awful hot – terrible! And they took out this ice cold water and he drank so much it just killed him.*[8] *'Course they couldn't do nothing, they just buried him... I suppose he'd be thirty or forty.*

Working for a lumber contractor also had the potential of bringing home much-needed cash. Johnnie A. MacLeod from Dell recalled his winters of working in a lumber-camp in the late 1920s when he learned that logging was a fairly miserable job, whereas there was 'real prestige' attached to the river drive. Johnnie, a Gaelic speaker, joined a camp crew, and found that he was the only fluent English speaker among eighty-five Frenchmen, all brought in for the woods operation.[9] Camp routine was fairly standard: the men slept in the one bunkhouse, heated by a central wood-burner and memorable for the bed-bugs, lice, body odour, and stifling atmosphere. 'Day' began at 3.30 a.m. with breakfast of beans, bread, and tea eaten outdoors. The first job was putting pulpwood into the river, ready for the drive. At 9 a.m. they stopped for the next meal, beans again. Back to work, tree after tree after tree was felled until lunch-time, at 2.30 p.m. – same as breakfast. Back to work till nightfall and the fourth meal of the day, a welcome plate of boiled beef and potatoes at the camp, again served outdoors. Back in the bunkhouse, despite fatigue, the men made their own entertainment of songs, stories, jokes and the occasional fiddle tune and step-dance, their only respite from a hard, dangerous and often lonely way of making a living.

They often went to bed wet, and always with their clothes on – a far cry from cutting peats and eating potatoes and herring back home in Lewis or Harris.

Snow comes early in that part of Canada, as I was to find out living in Quebec in 1976. The first snow fell on October 10th and it seemed to get deeper and deeper as the weeks went by. To my dismay, it was still melting in May and there was no such thing as 'daffodil time' or the joy of the first snowdrop. Yet, by the comfort of a warm stove, even when the village was cut off from the wider world by fifteen-foot snowdrifts, there was a peace and enjoyment in having time to listen to the experiences of the first few generations of Hebridean settlers.

Like many of the men, Alex MacIver learned to swing an axe from an early age. In the lumber woods he began working on the river drive in 1935, at the age of nineteen: 'I used to hire on for the log drives. And some of the drivers were younger than that. You'd pack your lunch and work for ten cents an hour for ten hours a day'. For Alex, as for most lumbermen, the bunkhouse songs and recitations were the most enjoyable part. It was a life that was fraught with danger and hardship and, as Russell recalled, for some families there was anguish and tragedy:

> *There's quite a knack in handling them logs in the water… There's some fellas could walk on them, and drive them, and ride them down the river. 'Course there's a lot of them got drowned too… There's a first cousin of my grandfather MacIver, Donald MacIver, same name, he came over from Loch Garvaig, and he just came over in time to go on the drive in spring… He didn't know anything at all about handling and stuff, you know, and he got drowned. He's*

> *buried in the MacIver cemetery. He was thirty years old, a nice fellow, strong and healthy. Yeah, there was a Tormod Matheson … he got killed by a tree … I think it's marked on the gravestone… And I think there was a Beaton in there got killed by a tree, a young fella. He was out with MacKenzie in Marsboro. Oh there's quite a few.*

A less dangerous way of earning a living was fox farming, which, in its hey-day, was a lucrative business for a few entrepreneurs. Duncan McLeod (whose grandfather was from Uig) was well acquainted with the 'fox men' as he and his boyhood companions used to enjoy their own small part in feeding locally bred silver foxes:

> *Well, the Mathesons, they had the big one – 1920, that's when Jimmy [Matheson] first got his breeding stock… And he bought this farm about half a mile out the road. Well, he kept say 250 or 300 females, and he had so many males to service them, and then first of all in the spring there would be more, probably 750 to 800, up to a thousand… And then there was some who kept just one or two or three. Well [the furs] were sold out of Montreal fur market, New York, and possibly in the London fur market… Oh, right after the Second World War, oh, 1947, 48 [the bottom dropped out of the market]…*
>
> *Well, [to feed them] when we'd catch rabbits we'd bring them to Jimmy, and he'd give us anywhere from 15 cents to 25 cents. Yeah, we'd trap them with snares.*

His friend Russell remembered a misadventure which, more than sixty years on, amused not only Russell but one of the other 'boys' involved:

We used to set snares for rabbits, and we'd sell the rabbits to the fox men – usually to Matheson's Silver Fox farm in Milan. And sometimes an owl would come along and he'd eat half of a rabbit, and we'd set a trap and he'd get caught. And we had two big horned owls at home one day, and Alex Campbell from Dell, he thought he'd like to have them. So he asked if he could have them, and we said 'Yeah, you can have them'. So he took them home and he put them in the hen house, and they killed all the hens! [Laughs!] Last time I saw Alex it was a few years ago, when Danny died… He asked if there was any deals going on with the owls yet! That was about sixty years ago since the owl incident.

Scarcely drawing breath, Russell continued:

One winter my father had a box-trap set for weasels,[10] *oh, the fur was worth something. One day, going to Milan, Murdo [Matheson] was ahead with a team [of horses] and we were behind with the other team. When he came down and he looked in and he yelled 'Tha sguireal agad!' [laughs, 'You have a squirrel']. So, they let the squirrel go… I used to catch a few of them – a dollar, and a dollar and a half. That was big money you know, for a young fella! There was a fellow from Sherbrooke used to come around… They'd buy hides… Oh they'd call here.*

Conversations about hunting, trapping and fishing could fill hours of entertainment as well as interest. In contrast to what their grandparents had left behind in the Outer Hebrides, where the men hunted *guga* and fished for *sgadad* but shooting deer or catching salmon was only for the privileged, there was a sense of freedom in Quebec, which soon became natural to them. Russell had a fund of stories most of which had a wry twist of humour. It was a way of life that he loved, as did his uncle Alex, who had gone 'out west' for a few years and ever after was known as *Alec Fiach* – 'wild Alex'.

Nicknames were as common in the Eastern Townships as in Lewis and Harris, similarly reflecting wit and amusement as well as history and sense of place. To mention but a few – there was a John MacArthur who went by the name of 'John Boston' because he had visited that city as a young man 'and couldn't stop talking about it'; Alex MacIver's uncle was known as 'The Bugler' (thought to have been associated with a stint in the army); John D. Graham was *Iain Domnhuill Aoghnais òg* [young John, son of Donald, son of Angus]; John K. MacLeod was *Iain Coinneach an t-saighdear* [John, son of Kenneth the soldier]; John MacKenzie was known as *Seonaidh a' Mhuillear* though he had never milled in his life, but 'inherited' the name from his grandfather who had been a miller in Tolsta. There was a family who all went by the name of *Sgoth* – far removed from the sea and a livelihood that depended upon fishing, but even after several generations they were known as this, the type of fishing craft used by their forebears who left Ness.

One family of MacAulays was referred to as *Sgaire*, or, more often than not, 'the Sgaires'. Having often heard the story from childhood, Muriel Mayhew (née MacDonald) explained that it was one of her father's relatives, Malcolm MacAulay, who emigrated from Lewis and settled on Bosta Hill. He was known as *Calum Sgaire* – Malcolm, son of Zachary.[11] He had been a fisherman and was in love with a young woman, Margaret MacLeod, from Bernera, where Muriel's mother had grown up:

> *My grandmother's ancestor, I suppose my ancestor too, was her aunt – of the Margaret in the story. Anyway they were*

lovers and they were supposed to get married and [as far as her parents were concerned] he was much beneath this family and they didn't want her to marry him because he was a sailor [fisherman], I guess. And he had come home, he had come back to get her, and they would go away together. And they had decided or planned to meet one particular night and she went out to meet him on the moors and a fog came up and she lost her way, and he thought she had decided not to come, and she, I guess, thought that he hadn't come to meet her, and then he made up the song after that, was what I was told. And his name was Malcolm and her name was Margaret, and he was Calum Sgaire [Malcolm, son of Zachary]. And in the end they made her marry a person they had chosen for her [the local merchant, an older man, with whom she would have a more prosperous life]. And she married him with her hands behind her back. She wouldn't give him her hand in marriage, and I think it was a few months or a year later she died. She was supposed to have died of a broken heart. Now isn't that romantic?

Later on I think he came to Canada [Quebec]. If I'm not mistaken, he married somebody else anyway – but he had made this song for her…

Ged is math a bhith seòòladh
'S olc a tha e 'gam chòrdadh
'S mór gum b'fheàrr a bhith 'm Bòsta
Cuir an eòrn' anns an raon.[12]

[Although it is good to be sailing/ It doesn't suit me at all/
I would far rather be in Bosta/ Planting the barley in the field].

To this day, Bosta (mentioned in the song) marks the place settled by MacAulays whose descendants are entirely French speaking today. Muriel's neighbour, Bill Young, whose people came from North Uist, added that in their young day (and even into the Fifties) 'some of the French spoke Gaelic too, you know'.

As Chris and Bill Lawson will testify, a visit with the descendants of the Quebec settlers in the Eastern Townships is very much like visiting in Lewis, Harris or any Hebridean island. The atmosphere is much like any informal *cèilidh* – the television is switched off, and, for the duration, simply does not exist. The kettle is scarcely boiled before the stories and reminiscences begin, with emotions running the full gamut, laughter to tears and often tears of laughter. There are stories of local characters, the wise, witty, foolish, brave or adventurous; the tragic life and death of Donald Morrison (the Megantic Outlaw)[13], cures or household hints; supernatural happenings suddenly emerge, though the story might start off, 'that time Peter MacRae was killed in the granite quarry…'. Ghost stories enough to make you nervous walking home might begin, 'when we were working in the woods…' or 'one time we were hunting…'. And, as many of the Township men had 'served King and country', there were many that began 'I remember during the war…'. The very mention of childhood Saturdays, however, was certain to light up the company with laughter and lively reminiscences such as on this occasion with Bill Young:

> *Saturday! Of course we had the well-house out back, you know, and we had the rope, with the bucket on the rope. We had to bring in the water; we had to bring in the wood… There was filling wood-boxes, splitting the kindling, piling*

the wood … that had to be all done the day before. Even the meals had to be prepared the day before. You might put the kettle on, or something like that, but the rest was ready. Cooking was put aside – [you'd hear] 'This pie is for Sunday; this cake is for Sunday; this cold meat's for Sunday'. Sunday there was nothing to be done.

The services were in Gaelic. And then, afterwards, they'd go home, and I had to go to Sunday School, and then I'd go home, and we'd all have dinner. And there'd be relations or somebody dropped in. They'd be all sitting quietly around on the verandah, or something, if the weather was good. And then, somebody would be elected to say a prayer, and we'd all have to go into the house, and we'd all have to get down – kneel down while prayers were said. And then in the evening, back we'd go to church. Now, you had to have something like an earthquake or the end of the world for to stay home from that! You had to go… A lot of people would come in from outlying districts and, especially in the morning service, they'd come in sleighs in the winter, and put their horses in sheds, and come in. Oh a storm never stopped them!

Differences between Lewis and Quebec landscape and weather aside, Saturday and Sunday kept all the routines of 'back home'. Only religious books were read on Sunday, though in some homes, this rule applied to every day of the week. Bill Young's grandmother was an enthusiastic reader of spiritual books, which seemed reason enough for her to decide on behalf of the entire family:

Well, it had to be religious, something religious. Oh, heavenly days! I remember the first Western story she ever caught me

> *with in the house! Well, I got rid of that fast – or she did! It wasn't on Sunday either! Whooosh! That was clear trash.*

Besides the observation of religious customs, the settlers also continued to celebrate seasonal customs, particularly Hallowe'en when, apart from guising, it was common to play pranks on neighbours or get up to some 'harmless' mischief on that special night. Ruth Nicolson (née MacDonald) recalled some of the things they got up to – usually the boys:

> *Like, they'd carry off your steps (if they were loose) and put them somewhere else. Or maybe the chairs on the front porch would disappear; they'd turn up again, and wherever they landed they would know who they belonged to. Or one time they put a buggy on top of the roof of a shed – that was the big boys – it'd have to be the big boys to handle that.*
>
> *Duncan D.L.'s grandfather, who had the store, was a very devoted temperance man, and, one Hallowe'en, a number of the young men, including his own son (Duncan), took tar and oil – black. And on the side of the store, next to the station – just across from the station, tracks in between – [they painted] D.L. McLEOD, SELLER OF LIQUORS. And almost every year as long as he lived, he painted it but that black oily paint would come through!*

As he listened to Ruth's story from fifty years ago, Duncan laughed as he brought it up to date: the graffiti outlived both his grandfather and his father and could still be seen when, finally, around 1992, Duncan himself had the old store torn down.

One of the social events that became popular in the Eastern Townships was the 'Box Social', when everyone, Gaels and French, would gather from miles around in support of a special cause. Christie and Johnnie MacKenzie (*Seonaidh a' Mhuillear*) of Scotstown remembered how common they once were, usually held in the school, though sometimes in a neighbour's home:

> *Anything happening, like the barn burning or the house burning or something [disastrous] – everybody pitched in and did what they could with the work and if there was anything they could give, they gave … it was just some way to help people… Oh, the Scotch and French, they'd hold together just the same … getting up box-socials to help. You know, selling the boxes and the proceeds going to a family that was destitute.*
>
> *It was an evening thing, and it would be all free, [no admission charge] for the neighbours … it was fun … and some of them boxes would be regular shoe-boxes, you know, all trimmed up. Inside was a lunch for two people – sandwiches and a cake and cookies, and sometimes fruit – whatever you could get. In the country store there wouldn't be too much variety… Some of them would be beautiful! And as a rule, the best trimmed ones brought the most money [regardless of what was inside] [laughs]. Well, of course, they wouldn't know what was inside till they were too late anyway – they'd have bought it! And they made tea or coffee [in the hall] – that was extra.*

Johnnie teasingly reminded Christie that 'the women made the boxes and the men were bidding on them – to get the women!' She smiled as she continued:

> *And you ate your lunch with your partner. Sometimes some had a mark on the box, you know, for their own girl, and the rest would make him pay for that box – they'd bid it, and*

bid it, and bid it up until – ! Yeah, it was fun... I remember my brother-in-law, Allan – he was going with a girl from Boston. She used to come to her grandparents' place for the summer. And my sister was home from Springhill, with her two girls. And the oldest girl wanted to go to a box-party, but she wanted Uncle Allan to buy her box because she didn't want a stranger to get her box. So Allan promised to do that, and when he started to bid on her box, everyone thought he had a mark on this Margaret MacIver's box, and they [pushed up the bidding as hard as they could] – he paid thirteen dollars to get that box! And it was his niece's box! [Laughs] But he wouldn't let her down, you know, he had promised to buy her box, and they kept on bidding against him... Two and a half or three dollars was usual ... that was since I can remember. Oh, yes, [it was a lot of money] but if somebody was in distress you gave what you could ... the money went to them.

Once in a while they'd have an orchestra [a band, to play for a dance]. The orchestra in them days was a violin player and a piano player, or an organ player. And they'd give them ten dollars – five dollars apiece for playing. Well, that came out of the proceeds, but the rest went to the night's cause.

Though Christie remembered details as if it had been only a week or two ago, she wistfully recalled that 'the last box-social I was at was in 1923'.

Quebec's Gaelic speakers refer to the month of April as *Mios an t-siùcair* [sugar month], as the first settlers soon learned that, when April arrived, they could expect to work six days a week extracting and processing maple sap for their main source of syrup and sugar. Tap a tree indeed! The reality is that it takes forty gallons of sap to make one gallon of syrup, not to mention further evaporation to make sugar. As the older generations look at the mechanised improvements that have turned this harvest into a world-famous market for Quebec, they look back on the days when they would spend 'all the hours of daylight God sent' tapping spigots into hundreds of maple trees to collect the sap in little tin pails. These were taken to the 'sugar house' (a *bothan* with a box stove and tin stove-pipe), emptied into a vat then boiled and stirred for hours and hours. Though the process was tediously long and demanding, at least the soaking wet clothes could dry out, painfully cold feet could be eased, and, best of all, the end product would be worth it.

At the end of April, with cans and bottles stored for the rest of the year, communities would hold a 'sugaring-off party'; similar to a 'harvest-home' this was a celebration for all the hard work of *Mios an t-siùcair*. Families would gather at the local hall on the appointed evening, and bring a sample of their season's syrup. They would then boil up the new syrups, and, when the experts judged it to be ready (the 'soft-ball test' in cold water), everyone would go outdoors and gather round the area of clean snow (usually near a fence where nobody had trodden) designated for the highlight of the night. Spectators were told to 'hold still' and 'keep clear' while competitors carried the boiling liquid out of the hall and lined up to throw it into the fresh snow. Instantly, it was turned into a kind of toffee, much to the delight of the youngsters in particular. Still outdoors, with fork in hand, everyone tucked in to the hard-earned treats, and 'if they were allowed', folk would return to the hall for the second part of the celebration, usually a dance.

Not all families approved of this part, as Maryann Morrison (Angus's mother) experienced when her father forbade dancing, because his generation were under the impression that Christ Himself preached against it. Scriptural references to 'King David dancing before the Lord' seem of no relevance to any allegation that dancing was condemned by Christ, as Muriel confirmed: 'I can remember a minister who said if you went to a dance and you thought the Lord was with you He'd leave you at the door! So much for "I will be with you always, even unto the ends of the earth"'.

Nevertheless, the acknowledgement of a spiritual aspect in every area of life was, and is, as deeply significant among the Gaels in Quebec as in the Hebrides. 'In all things give thanks' meant that, even if invited out for afternoon tea, not a sip would be drunk till all heads were bowed and grace said. Until the 1990s it could still be heard in Gaelic, '*Tha sinn a' toirt taing dhuit, a Thighearna, air son na cothraman prìseil so tha thu buileachadh oirnn...*' (We give thee thanks, oh Lord, for the precious gifts bestowed on us...). Biblical Proverbs a-plenty provided appropriate words for every occasion and personality trait, at best used with kindness, wisdom and in the spirit of encouragement, all much needed as the community worked together in almost every facet of life.

Today there are no Gaelic church services and, to the regret of the few Presbyterian congregations that are left, the small village churches rapidly decline annually. In 1976, little did I imagine that the Gaelic church service I recorded (led by the Rev. Donald Gillies of St. Kilda) would be the last, or that fifteen years later the church itself would be 'torn down' – better than it turning into a bingo hall, was the thinking at the time. It was not a decision that had any input from the local Catholic population, by far in the majority. By way of contrast, however, in the early 1990s, when another local community church faced closure, the very suggestion that this little, wooden Presbyterian church, 'Chalmers Church', was destined to be sold or demolished, evoked instant response – it must be saved. Few of those who saved it were familiar with the name of Chalmers, however, as the majority were Catholic, who, out of an immeasurable respect for the first settlers, carefully moved it to a new location in the village of Gould. Since 1999 it has been the focus of cultural and spiritual visits – walk through the door and you are likely to hear the sound of the Gaelic psalm, albeit from a recorded source, but still the authentic sound of the Gaelic settlers. Visitors are told (in French) that their tour begins here so that people will not only hear about the history and way of life of the Gaelic settlers but, more importantly, reflect on the deep faith that nurtured and sustained them.

The legacy of the first settlers can be seen the length and breadth of the Eastern Townships, even though there are now so few Gaelic speakers left that, alas, they could be counted on one hand. Most of the descendants of the pioneer settlers from Lewis, Harris and North Uist now speak French, and, like their forebears, learn English after they go to school. The scope of this paper cannot address the important issues of language use and loss (both of which I have discussed elsewhere) but hopefully gives some insight into the lives of the first settlers – those who emigrated from the Outer Isles.

As time passes, there are fewer and fewer to tell their story, but, far from fading into oblivion, it has a vibrant interest today, particularly among those who live on the old farms or in nearby villages. Many have no connection with the area whatsoever but move there either because land and house prices are favourable or simply to escape from the city. As Quebec is Canada's French province, newcomers are initially surprised to hear that their farmland was first cleared by hard working immigrants from Scotland. Even in the 1970s I was asked '*Nouvelle Écosse?*' (Nova Scotia?) and, when the issue of language was raised, there was disbelief in the exclamation, '*les anglais qui ne parlaitent l'anglais!*' (English people who don't speak English!). Quick to share local history, many seek out the 'original' family that connects them to Scotland.[14]

For more than a decade there have been festivals and events in the Eastern Townships paying tribute to the Gaelic setters. In scale they range between *Homage aux Premiers Arrivants Écossais* (A Homage to the First Scottish Settlers), attracting 8,000 people to a three-day event, to small, invited regular lectures (usually in French) at local universities, colleges, schools, societies and museums. There are also food-related experiences in a local restaurant dedicated to *les traditions des Écossais* where folk stop for tea and *des scones et des oatcakes*, made by the local chef, Daniel Audet, who has visited the Outer Hebrides to taste the sea air, as well as the food – some members of *Comann Eachdraidh Nis* remember him from 1999. The recipes he uses in the Eastern Townships are not from Lewis, however, but from the direct descendants of emigrants, such as Ruth Nicolson, Muriel Mayhew and the generation who learned from their mothers and grandmothers. This is the true taste of the Eastern Townships, reflecting not only the 'old country' but also the new, with slight adaptations suited to the produce of Quebec.[15] Besides, there were many new tastes that became incorporated into the diets of the Gaels so quickly that even Angus Morrison, only one generation removed from Harris, thought that beans and buckwheat grew there as readily as oats or potatoes.

In 2005, a group of dedicated enthusiasts set up the new *Centre Culturel Oscar Dhu* (Oscar Dhu Cultural Centre) in an upstairs room above the restaurant. The non-profit organisation promotes Eastern Township culture through a range of events and activities interpreting the history and traditions of the Gaelic settlers. It is remarkable that a small village of scarcely thirty houses can make such an impact both regionally and nationally, as visitors come from considerable distances to take part or even to spend a night or two at 'Maison Macaulay'. Restored to all its Victorian elegance, it is now a B & B, which has even been celebrated by *Châtelaine Magazine*. Visitors will not find 'TV in every room' (or indeed in any room), nor even an *ensuite* bathroom, but they will find what they are looking for: a home furnished in the style of the '*les habitants Écossais*', beds with hand-stitched patchwork quilts, lace curtains, glass lamps, old photographs, classic books and a myriad of reminders of the past. Best of all, they will find peace and quiet, time to reflect or simply to get away from it all.

The adjacent restaurant, with Saltire and Lion Rampant flying over the door, speaks of Scotland before you walk through the door and overhear animated conversations in French. It may not be the tartan tablecloths that evoke acute nostalgia for the 'old country', but more the bone china teacups and saucers, the smell of scones and taste of homemade jam – the real reminders of the Scotland we knew and loved (I found myself asking when was the last time I made scones as I swithered between the rabbit stew and venison casserole). Daniel has kept the original kitchen range and his menu offers dishes from a contented past, when there were no microwaves, no boil-in-the-bag, no oven-readies, no 'additives', no carry-outs and the word 'organic' was yet to be invented. There was basic, homegrown, simply prepared, nutritious old-fashioned cooking, the kind that Maryann Morrison summed up when asked, 'However did you survive the first winter?'

'My dear,' she replied, 'we had oatmeal and the catechism'. Food for the body, food for the soul; neglect either at your peril. More than a hundred years on, it is the value system of the early settlers that draws today's generation whose lifestyle epitomises pressure and tension. They sense a contentedness and moral fabric that once characterised the lives of the pioneer settlers and so they come in search of qualities that are hard to find in the fast pace of the modern world. Perhaps, in tasting their food, listening to their music and their language, learning about their history and way of life, the essence of it all may rub off, even for a few days.

Reflecting on the conference in Harris, few would deny that The Islands Book Trust provided all of these qualities for those initially drawn to the theme, 'Emigration from the Outer Hebrides'. Attendees may not have set out to 'get away from it all' but most found that the three-day gathering turned out to be as much an experience as a conference. There were deeply moving testimonies of islanders whose people lived through the actual emigration; there was an opportunity to visit cleared districts, to stand and gaze at the emptiness and imagine the sound of children playing. And there were more than a few conversations that looked back (with nostalgia) to a time when islanders knew a different way of life.

While Homecoming Scotland 2009 will be remembered as a year of clan and family reunions it will also mark the discovery of new links. As the year draws to a close, the Scottish Government's Diaspora Forum is already planning the follow-up, to 'create a really significant and long-lasting legacy of Homecoming Scotland 2009',[16] to continue to build 'links across the seas'[17] and to use the Diaspora Forum as 'a chance to recapture that history and magic'.[18]

Meanwhile, back in the Eastern Townships, the September 2009 'What's on' brochure (or its equivalent) listed several events, all Scottish. The main attraction was *Céilidh Échos d'Écosse*, a multi-media piece about the Eastern Township pioneer settlers, with narrative, songs (some in Gaelic), music, dance and visual interpretations. The stage setting is '*dans le taigh-céilidh, la «maison des histoires», contes, poèmes, anecdotes, proverbes, chansons, musique ... dans l'esprit de la légendaire hospitalité des Écossais originaires des Highlands*'.

Even for the non-French speaker, words and expression stand out, such as *taigh-céilidh* (retaining the acute accent), aptly and beautifully conveyed by *la maison des histories* [with legends, poems, anecdotes, proverbs, songs, music ... in the spirit of the legendary hospitality of the original Scottish Highlanders].

People who have never seen the sea, far less Scotland, are drawn to the 'story' and traditions of the Eastern Townships' pioneer settlers from the Outer Hebrides. Driving through miles of dense forest, with adjacent farms carved out of a wilderness, it is hard to imagine what it would be like if there were not a single tree in sight. What would it be like to sit by a peat fire? Where does peat grow? Does it blaze and crackle like wood and is it hard to split?

The only way to find out would be to visit *les îles de Lewis, Harris et Uist* and to seek out a real peat fire. Already there are plans afoot to 'bring a taste of Quebec' back home to share with the descendants of the first settlers. Daniel Audet plans to take a break from his own kitchen and bring traditional Quebec foods to Scotland so that he can prepare a meal for the descendants of the Gaelic settlers. Had it not been for buckwheat, beans and maple syrup as well as 'wild meats' there would be fewer Morrisons, MacArthurs,

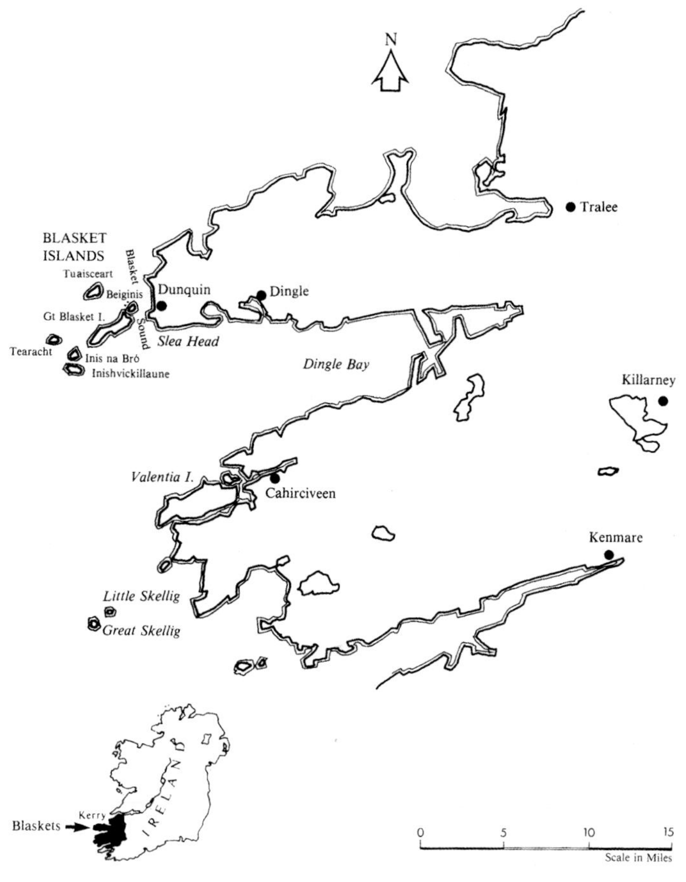

A map of south-west Ireland showing the location of the Blasket Islands (Mícheál de Mórdha)

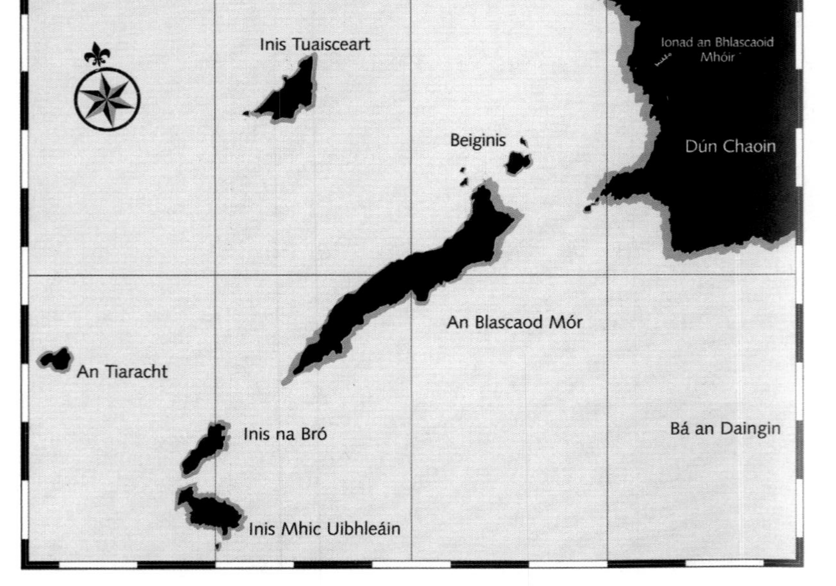

A map of the Blasket archipelago showing the Irish Gaelic names for the islands and also the location for the Blasket Centre on the mainland (Mícheál de Mórdha)

The American Dream! The most westerly point on Great Blasket, Ceann Dubh (Black Head), with a superimposed photograph of the 1930s Manhattan skyline. From Great Blasket Centre exhibition (Mícheál de Mórdha)

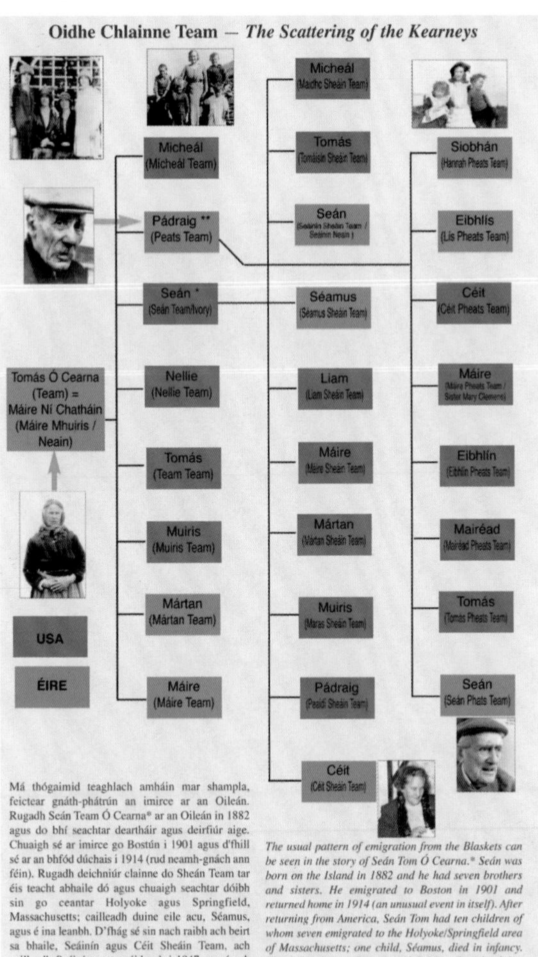

Oidhe Chlainne Team — The Scattering of the Kearneys
Tomás Ó Cearna (Team) = Máire Ní Chatháin (Máire Mhuiris / Neain)
USA
ÉIRE
Micheál (Mícheál Team)
Pádraig ** (Peats Team)
Seán * (Seán Team/Ivory)
Nellie (Nellie Team)
Tomás (Team Team)
Muiris (Muiris Team)
Mártan (Mártan Team)
Máire (Máire Team)
Micheál (Maidhc Sheáin Team)
Tomás (Tomáisín Sheáin Team)
Seán (Seáinín Sheáin Team / Seáinín Neain)
Séamus (Séamus Sheáin Team)
Liam (Liam Sheáin Team)
Máire (Máire Sheáin Team)
Mártan (Mártan Sheáin Team)
Muiris (Maras Sheáin Team)
Pádraig (Peaidí Sheáin Team)
Céit (Céit Sheáin Team)
Siobhán (Hannah Pheats Team)
Eibhlís (Lís Pheats Team)
Céit (Céit Pheats Team)
Máire (Máire Pheats Team / Sister Mary Clemens)
Eibhlín (Eibhlín Pheats Team)
Mairéad (Mairéad Pheats Team)
Tomás (Tomás Pheats Team)
Seán (Seán Phats Team)
Má thógaimid teaghlach amháin mar shampla, feictear gnáth-phátrún an imirce ar an Oileán. Rugadh Seán Team Ó Cearna* ar an Oileán in 1882 agus do bhí seachtar deartháir agus deirfiúr aige. Chuaigh sé ar imirce go Bostún i 1901 agus d'fhill sé ar an bhfód dúchais i 1914 (rud neamh-gnách ann féin). Rugadh deichniúr clainne do Sheán Team tar éis teacht abhaile dó agus chuaigh seachtar dóibh sin go ceantar Holyoke agus Springfield, Massachusetts; cailleadh duine eile acu, Séamus, agus é ina leanbh. D'fhág sé sin nach raibh ach beirt sa bhaile, Seáinín agus Céit Sheáin Team, ach cailleadh Seáinín go tragóideach i 1947 gan é ach cúig bliana fichead.
Arís eile, rugadh ochtar leanbh do dheartháir Sheáin Team, Pádraig** (Peats Team); caill an eitinn duine acu, Éibhlís, ina hóige agus thug Céit, Máire, Eibhlín, Máiréad agus Tomás faoin imirce. Níor fhan ach beirt in Éirinn.
Eolas bailithe ó Ghinealach an Bhlascaoid, i Leabharlann Ionad an Bhlascaoid Mhóir.
The usual pattern of emigration from the Blaskets can be seen in the story of Seán Tom Ó Cearna.* Seán was born on the Island in 1882 and he had seven brothers and sisters. He emigrated to Boston in 1901 and returned home in 1914 (an unusual event in itself). After returning from America, Seán Tom had ten children of whom seven emigrated to the Holyoke/Springfield area of Massachusetts; one child, Séamus, died in infancy. That left only two, Seáinín and Céit, on the Island, but Seáinín died tragically in 1947 at the early age of 25 years.
Similarly, Seán Tom's brother, Pádraig** (Peats Tom), who had eight children: Eibhlís died in infancy of tuberculosis and Céit, Máire, Eibhlín, Máiréad and Tomás emigrated. Only two remained in Ireland.
Information collected from the Blasket Genealogy in the Library of the Blasket Heritage Centre.

A chart showing the pattern of emigration in the family of Tom Ó Cearna of Great Blasket and that of one of his sons, Pádraig Ó Cearna (Peats Tom Ó Cearna). The purple colour denotes those who emigrated and the green colour denotes those who stayed in Ireland. Chart by Feargal Mac Amhlaoibh; from Great Blasket Centre exhibition (Mícheál de Mórdha)

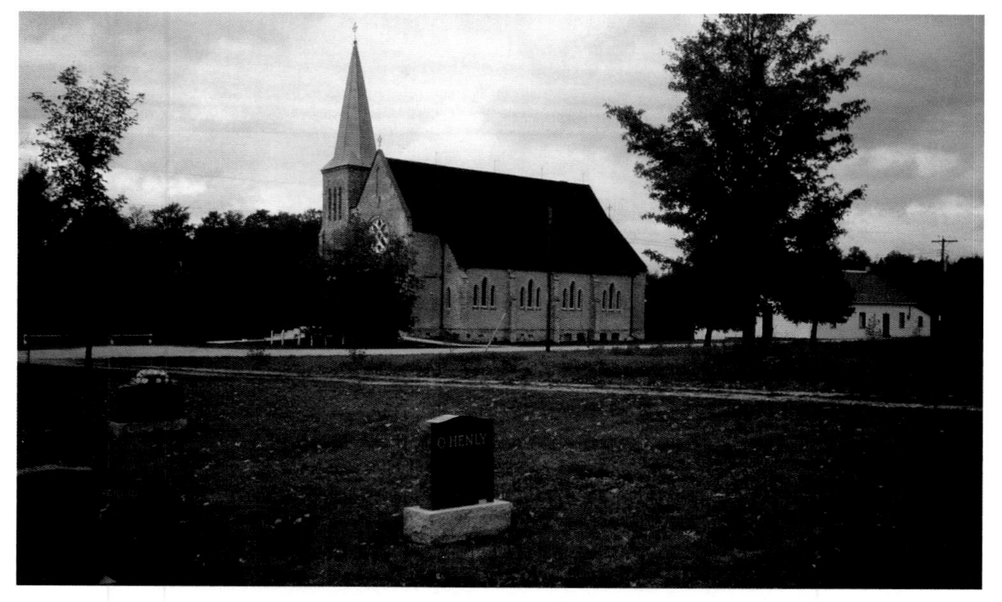

Graveyard at Tracadie Cross, Prince Edward Island (Bill Lawson)

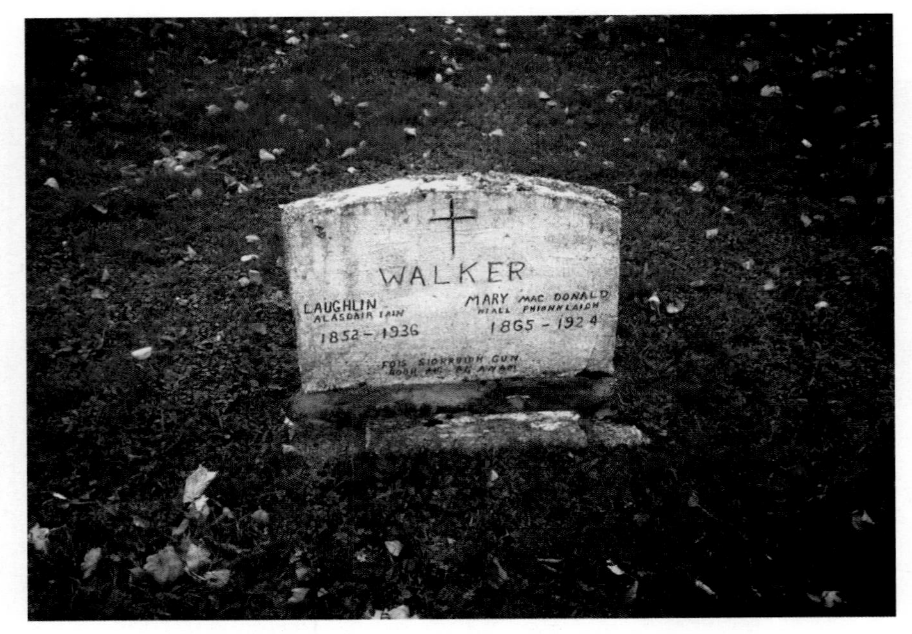

West Lake Ainslie, Cape Breton Island (Bill Lawson)

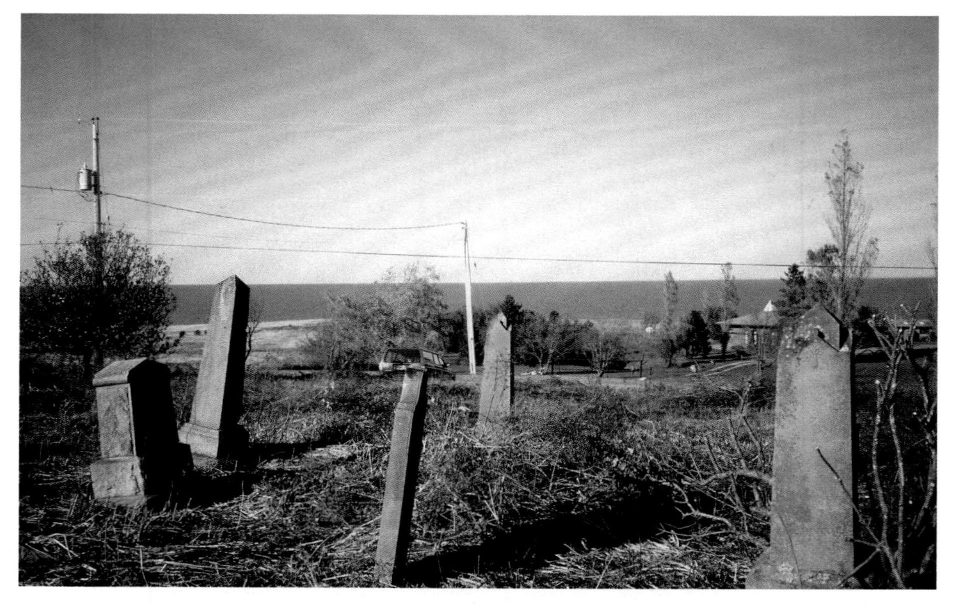

Lewis Cemetery, Gulf Shore, Nova Scotia (Bill Lawson)

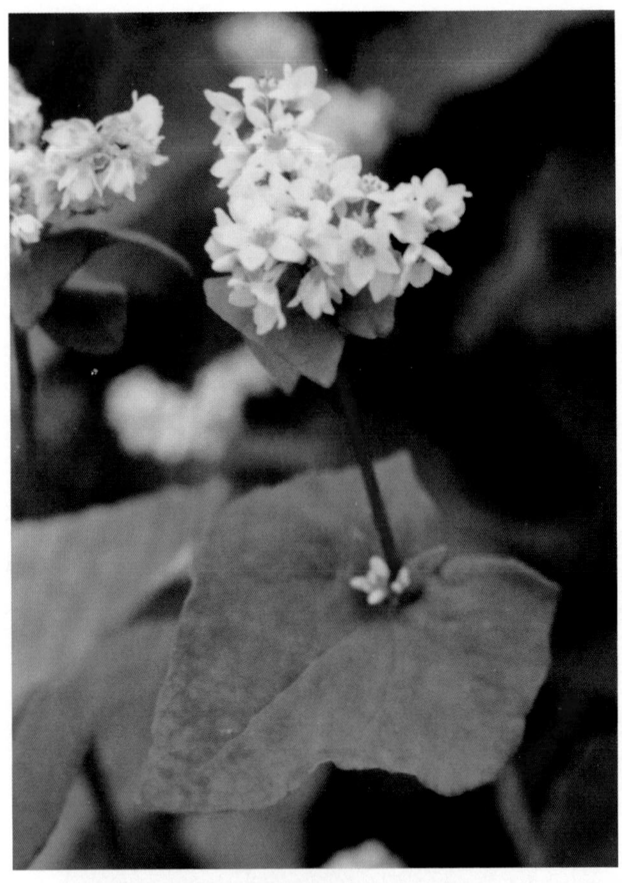

Buckwheat in flower (Margaret Bennett)

The men of the Gaelic congregation, after Communion Service, outside Marsboro Church, 1919 (Margaret Bennett)

Donald Morrison, wanted as 'the Megantic Outlaw'
(Margaret Bennett)

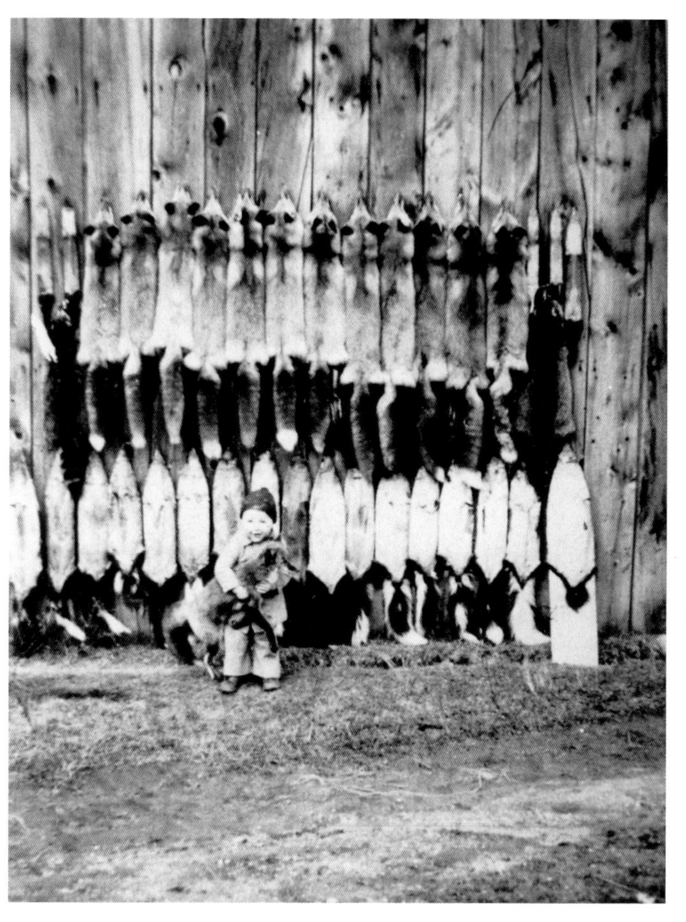

Fox farm in the Eastern Townships (Margaret Bennett)

Stornoway town sign, Eastern Townships, Canada (Chris Lawson)

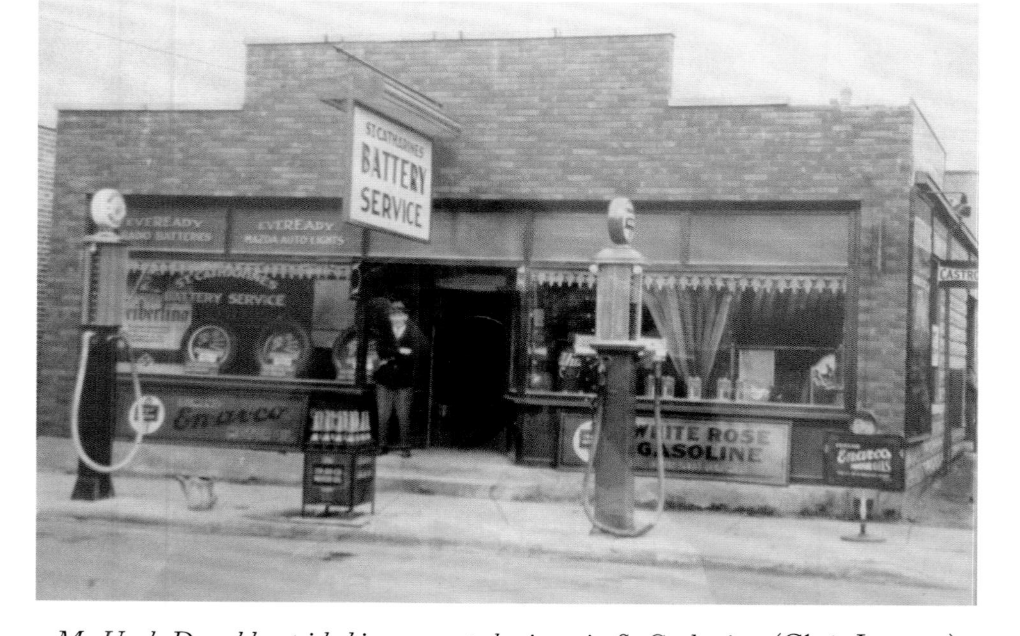

My Uncle Donald outside his new auto business in St Catharines (Chris Lawson)

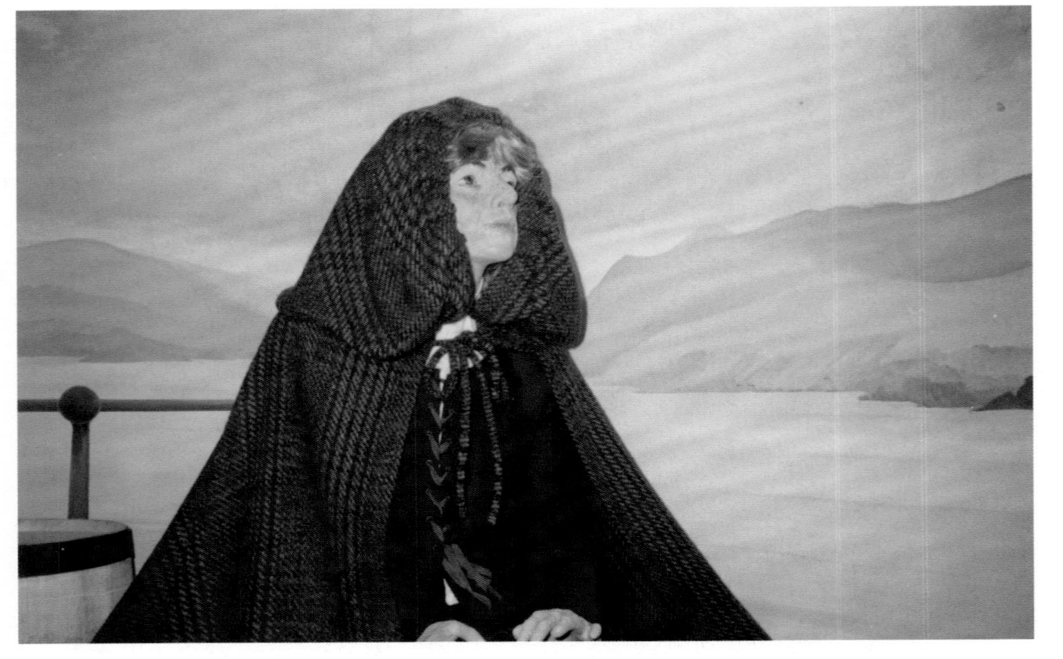

Model of an emigrant leaving Scotland, Hector Museum, Pictou, Nova Scotia (Chris Lawson)

Bill Lawson at Cape North Museum, Cape Breton. Many emigrants from Pabbay, Harris, settled here after the clearance of the island in 1846 (Chris Lawson)

The wool-laden wagons headed from far inland to the waiting cargo vessels in Rio Gallegos and Punta Arenas (Greta Mackenzie)

A modern road now runs through the pampa (Greta Mackenzie)

View over the pampa (Greta Mackenzie)

A Tehuelche family in Rio Gallegos, Argentina in the early 1900s (Greta Mackenzie)

A bronze life-size monument erected in memory of the shepherds in Punta Arenas
(Greta Mackenzie)

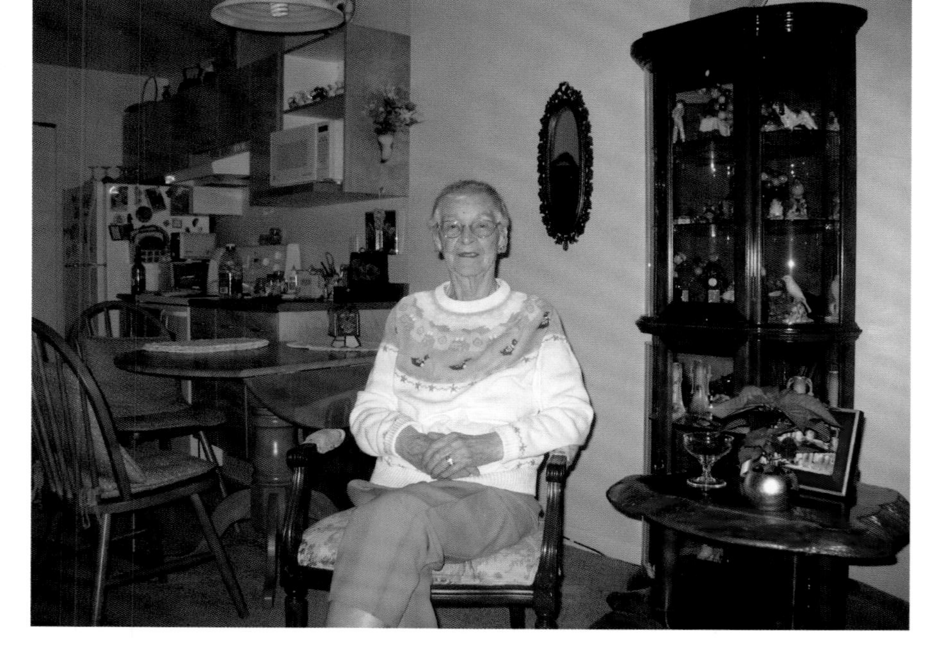

The late Morag Bennett (Permission to reproduce image granted by her son)

Murdo Macivor (Courtesy of Murdo Macivor)

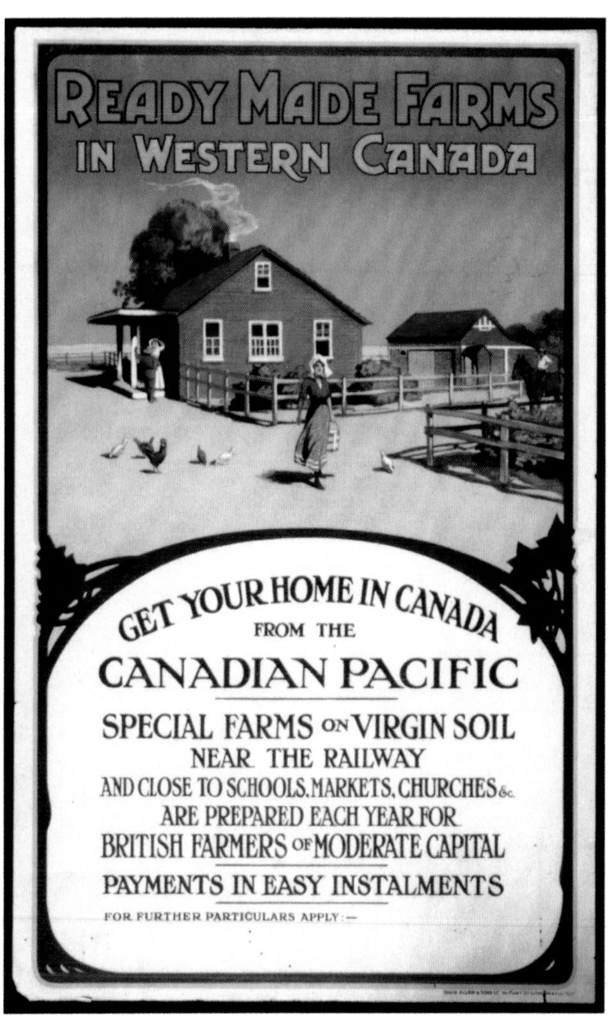

Print from Library and Archives Canada: 'Ready Made Farms in Western Canada – get your home in Canada from the Canadian Pacific' (Marjory Harper)

Canadian Immigration Offices in Inverness decorated for visit of Duke and Duchess of York, May 1929 (Marjory Harper)

MacDonalds, MacLeods, Stewarts, Nicolsons and Beatons in Quebec today – they might all have starved during their first winter.

Bibliography

Bennett, Margaret. *Oatmeal and the Catechism: Scottish Gaelic Settlers in Quebec*, John Donald, Edinburgh, and McGill-Queen's, Montreal. 2nd edition, with *Postscript*, Birlinn, Edinburgh, 1998 and 2003.

Bennett, Margaret. 'Cultural Changes in Quebec since the Gaelic Settlers', *Island Notes*, The Islands Book Trust, Lewis, 2008.

Bennett, Margaret. 'Gaelic Song in Eastern Canada: Twentieth Century Reflections', in *Folksongs: Chansons, Ottawa: Canadian Folklore Canadien*, Vol. 14, No. 2, pp. 21–34, 1992.

Bennett, Margaret. 'One and Two Percent: Scottish Gaelic Folklore Studies in Newfoundland and Quebec', Proceedings from the conference *FOLKLORE 150*, in *Lore and Language*, Vol. 15, No. 1–2, Sheffield, pp. 128–140, 1996.

Bennett, Margaret. 'From the Quebec-Hebrideans to "les Ecossais-Québecois": Tracing the Evolution of a Scottish Cultural Identity in Canada's Eastern Townships', in Celeste Ray, *Highland Heritage: Scottish Americans in the American South*, Chapel Hill and London, 2001.

Epps, Bernard. *The Outlaw of Megantic*, Toronto, 1973.

Kidd, Henry G. *The Megantic Outlaw*, Toronto, 1948.

Lawson, Bill. *A Register of Emigrant Families from the Western Isles of Scotland to the Eastern Townships of Quebec, Canada*, Compton County Historical Museum Society, Eaton Corner, Quebec, 1998.

MacKay, Angus (Oscar Dhu). *Donald Morrison, the Canadian Outlaw: A Tale of the Scottish Pioneers*, n.p., 1892. Reprint (1965, 1975) Sherbrooke. Enhanced Centennial Edition (1993), introduced by Thomas A. McKay, Arlington.

MacLeod, Finlay/Fionnlagh MacLeòid. *Muilnean Beaga Leòdhais/ The Norse Mills of Lewis*, illustrated by John Love, *Acair*, Stornoway, 2009.

Mathieu, André. *Donald et Marion*, Saint-Eustache, Quebec, 1990.

Morrison, Hugh Mackenzie. 'The Principles of Free Grants in the Land Act of 1841', in *Canadian Historical Review*, University of Toronto Press, Vol. 14, No. 4, 1933.

Wallace, Clarke. *Wanted – Donald Morrison: The True Story of the Megantic Outlaw*, Toronto, 1977.

Notes

1. Shefford, Stanstead and Sherbrooke.
2. The scheme was part of the Land Act of 1841. Later the offer was a hundred acres.
3. All quotations from speech are from verbatim transcriptions of my fieldwork recordings made in the Eastern Townships between 1976 and 2002.
4. Donald MacDonald, *The Tolsta Townships*, p. 148, and *Lewis: A History of the Island*, p. 78.
5. Though none are in use today, some operated till the 1940s. The restoration of the Swainbost mill (as a museum) shows visitors the ingenuity of the technology. More than 250 sites of mills have been identified in Lewis, many dating back several centuries; see Finlay MacLeod, *The Norse Mills of Lewis*, illustrated by John Love.
6. One of the descendants, Alphonse Legendre, was recorded for the project. See Guy Lalumière et al., *Stornoway 1858–1983, Les Albums Souvenirs Québecois*, Sherbrooke, 1983, p. 165. See also photographs of the site, and of subsequent mills, pp. 31–32. TRANSLATION: The Legendre brothers had the first saw-mill, built by Donald McLeod who constructed several mills in the region.
7. See *Oatmeal and the Catechism*, p. 19.

8. Part of the advice given to emigrants (written in the pamphlets distributed on embarkation) was that new settlers should avoid drinking large quantities of ice-cold water as it could induce shock and even death.
9. John Austin MacLeod (Johnnie Bard), *Memoirs of Dell*, unpubl. ms., Kingston, 1971, pp. 191–193.
10. This is a simply made, rectangular wooden box with a trigger device inside that releases a sliding door, which, when set, is suspended over the opening. Common in many parts of Canada and America. See Henry Glassie, *Pattern in the Material Folk Culture of the Eastern United States*, Philadelphia, 1968, p. 169, Fig. 49.
11. According to Dr Donald MacDonald, the name Zachary [*Sgaire*] is peculiar to the MacAulays of Uig; *Tales and Traditions of the Lews*, p. 58. He also refers to a Zachary MacAulay, tacksman of Valtos in 1712, indicating the longevity of the MacAulay connection (pp. 42–43).
12. A version of the story of Margaret MacLeod and Malcolm MacAulay was recorded by Francis Collinson in Bernera, Lewis, in 1954. See also *Tocher*, 9, pp. 34–35, though there is no mention of Malcolm going to Quebec.
13. In 1976 I tape-recorded Morrison's niece, Christy MacArthur, who was a little girl when he died and also Maryann Morrison who, as a teenager, used to be sent out to the sugar bush with food for Donald. I did not, however, hear the entire story at any one time, but had to piece it together from many sessions, with 'gaps' filled in by reading biographic works such as Kidd and Epps.
14. To cite one example: Peter Jort (of Swedish extraction) moved from Montreal with no inkling that the farm he had bought had been cleared by a MacDonald family and the house built by Ruth Nicolson's grandfather. He knew that the area had 'great skiing' and land was cheap. He soon became a regular visitor at Ruth's house and thirty years on is a fund of knowledge about the early settlers.

15. Even today, British immigrants in Canada quickly find out that Canadian flour is not the same as that produced 'at home' – the gluten content differs so significantly that recipes that work successfully with British flour will not produce the same results with Canadian flour (and vice versa). Recipes have to be adjusted, usually a trial and error process, if the expert scone-maker hopes to attain success.
16. Culture Minister Michael Russell MSP at the launch of the Diaspora Forum.
17. Rt. Hon. George Reid, MSP (launch speech).
18. Rt. Hon. the Lord (David) Steel of Aikwood (launch speech).

6

Gaelic Emigrants to Canada

Chris Lawson

'To my mother and father I owe the gift of my native tongue.' So wrote Sister Margaret McDonnell, formerly head of Celtic Studies at St Francis Xavier University in Antigonish in Nova Scotia, in the acknowledgements in her book of emigrant songs, *The Emigrant Experience*.[1] Margaret McDonnell is many generations removed from Scotland but her passion for the language of her ancestors from Eigg and Colonsay became very evident when she spoke to me in Antigonish in the early 1990s.

Canada was a big part of my life growing up as many of my family had emigrated there, mainly in the very early 1920s. One of my earliest memories is of my Uncle Donald arriving home after a break of twenty-nine years away from Lewis. He had married and set up home and a business in the Niagara area and did not often meet Gaelic speakers. His wife was of Germanic origin and Gaelic was not the language of their home. He decided it was time to come home to Lewis to see his elderly mother but had to ask for her forbearance when he tried to speak Gaelic after so many years away.

Each summer in Point in Lewis, a stream of Canadian visitors came and went, visiting relatives. There were many invitations to visit them and letters flew back and fore all the time, so Canada was a place we knew better than we knew other places in Lewis.

In 1989, when I first visited Canada, I suppose I had preconceived ideas about the country but they were soon dispelled, especially in Quebec. It was on my first visit to the Eastern Townships of Quebec that I became aware of the Gaelic language, where it was still the native language of some people, just around thirty or so then. With a good friend of my husband's, Muriel Mayhew, who was in her early eighties, I was taken along the Scotch Road, Bury, to the ruins of houses, and listened as they spoke of who had lived in them: *Taigh Iomhair*, *Taigh nam Peutanaich*, all Lewis and Gaelic names. This was an aspect of history I did not know much about although Scotstown was a town known to us, as my great grandmother's sister had gone to live there when she married the man known as the *Innseanach*, the Indian. He was given the nickname after having been in the service of the Hudson's Bay Company and had returned to Lewis twice before eventually settling in Canada and the United States with his family.

Muriel took us to see Christie MacArthur, who was 104 years old. Christie was a niece of Donald Morrison, the Megantic Outlaw. In a hospital in Lac Megantic, she spoke to me of memories of the old folk of the Eastern Townships. She and I spoke Gaelic, much to the interest of the mainly French-speaking staff. It was there that my interest in the remnants of the Gaelic speakers of Canada was really aroused. When I came back to Harris I was telling Donald Alasdair Stewart from Back about the people I had met and he asked if I had taped them. I then contacted Jo MacDonald at Radio nan Gaidheal and she arranged to give me recording equipment when I went out later in 1990. I recorded hours of conversations with people in the Eastern Townships and brought them back to Jo in Stornoway who edited the numerous tapes into an hour-long programme called *Le Làmhach agus Bìobail*, *With Axe and Bible*, a quote from Christie Mackenzie, one of the people whose Gaelic was as fluent as mine.

I picked various pieces from interviews for the Emigration Conference, starting in the Eastern Townships of Quebec. These featured Johnnie Mackenzie, *Seonaidh Mhurchaidh a' Mhuilleir*, then ninety-nine years of age. Seonaidh told me about buckwheat and the pancakes they made with it. Muriel Mayhew spoke of how her mother came from Lewis to work for a cousin, a minister from Lacasaidh in Lochs. There were no proper roads then and she was sure she would not stay there but stay she did. I then played an extract from the conversations with Angus and Eva Morrison in Megantic, a brother and sister whose parents had come from Harris in the 1880s. Angus and Eva were full of stories and fun and sang the memorable song relating the tale of Barney Google. Eva told of the first radio in the area and how they put the headphones in the milk can to enhance the sound!

In the Cladach a Tuath, North Shore, Cape Breton, we met the amazing John Shaw, a member of the Cape Breton Singers whose singing we knew from radio programmes back home in Scotland. In Cape Breton in the early 1990s it was said that there were 1,000 people whose first language was Gaelic. Now figures of around 500 to 1,000 are given although in a business plan drawn up by the Office of Gaelic Affairs in Nova Scotia the numbers there are thought to be around 2,000.[2] In the mid 1800s Gaelic was thought to be the third most spoken language along with Irish Gaelic in Canada after English and French.

In Wreck Cove, Cape Breton, high above the edge of the Atlantic, where I imagined large sailing ships arriving from Scotland with emigrants, I met Alex Smith, Evelyn and Annie Mae. Alex was descended from folk who emigrated from my own home village of Sheshader in the very early 1800s before the village was broken into crofts. Their accent was quite different to that of John Shaw's, further down the coast, who said his people were from the island of Berneray. His people left the Hebrides in the early 1800s as well and yet his accent told you where his roots were.

John Shaw needed little prompting when it came to singing a song, and his renderings of *Fhir a' Bhàta* and *Ho ro mo nighean donn bhoidheach* are particularly fine. His hand kept time on the kitchen table as he sang. I was amazed to hear the same songs and tunes in Cape Breton as those we knew in the islands although the words were adapted often to fit the life in Canada. Many of the songs were adapted to the style used for waulking the tweed. John Shaw said the men did the waulking and at performances of waulking later we attended sessions where this was the case although women were invited if they were good and willing singers.

On mainland Nova Scotia I had the privilege of meeting and recording conversations with Professor Kenneth Nilsen and Sister Margaret McDonnell. Margaret McDonnell's first language was Gaelic and she was responsible for a major collection of Gaelic books and papers which are held at St Francis Xavier University. She worked along with Professor Calum I. MacLeod on the collection and later with Dr John Shaw on folklore collections. Professor Kenneth Nilsen is of Norwegian and Irish descent but a fluent Scottish Gaelic speaker. He became interested in Scottish Gaelic while he was in Boston.

Mary Jane Lamont, now a well-known Gaelic singer with an international reputation, I met while she was still a student at St Francis Xavier University. Mary Jane's family left North Uist in the 1820s and she grew up in Montreal. Summers were spent in Cape Breton with relatives and there her obvious love of the Gaelic language and the traditional songs had started her off on a career which has taken her to Scotland many times, the first of those trips to Harris where she and my husband presented an unforgettable programme based on the people and the songs of Nova Scotia. It fascinated us that she could have her choruses picked up and sung by a Scottish audience.

While she was here she heard the singing of Donald MacDonald of Horgabost, one of the great traditional song bearers of the Hebrides, and after he sang a song written by Eachain a' Mhuilich from Berneray, Mary Jane told the audience that the last time she had heard that song was on her tape recorder the previous night, sung by someone from the North Shore in Cape Breton! I could see that she was having the same reaction as I had experienced in her homeland.

We also met people like Joe Murphy who had learnt Gaelic. Joe's people had come from Ireland and he was brought up in Ontario. When he went to Nova Scotia he believed Gaelic was a dead language until he heard it spoken on local radio by Rosemary McCormack, a lady from South Uist who had emigrated to Canada. I had long conversations with Rosemary in the early 1990s about how she viewed the state of Gaelic in Canada. Although she was doing so much to encourage the language herself she was quite pessimistic as to its future. Rosemary said that she believed the day you found it difficult to get your own children to speak Gaelic, you were beginning to lose the battle. She had a six-year-old child then whose first language was Gaelic but who found it strange that the only people who spoke Gaelic to her mother were old people!

In Prince Edward Island I met the last native Gaelic speaker. Rev. Donald Nicolson lived in Cornwall and while my husband lectured at a seminar in Charlottetown, I set off to meet this remarkable man. I had spoken to him on the telephone and by the time I got to his house he had gathered around him all his Scottish memorabilia. There were photographs of his own family, books and Bibles but although he had said he was a Gaelic speaker his ability to converse in the language had vanished over the years. His grandfather had insisted that his older brother, Neil, learnt Gaelic as he was sure to learn English anyway. Neil had lived in New York but had been dead for many years, leaving Donald with little opportunity to speak Gaelic to anyone. 'I can sing and tell stories,' he told me and so he did. His Gaelic hymns were the ones my mother sang in our home in Lewis – *Air a' Chrann* and *O! Miorbhail Gràis*.

His people had emigrated from Ronay and Raasay early in the nineteenth century. He and his father had worked in the woods of Ontario with Tormod Mòr MacDonald from Upper Bayble and he had visited his son, Neil, in Bayble. He had a Bible that Neil and his wife had given to him. On that visit he was accompanied by his grandson and he took him to Raasay. Donald was concerned about what the grandson's impressions of Raasay would be and as they left he asked him what he thought of the island and the visit. The grandson replied, 'As we left my eyes were wet with tears'.

The area I recorded in most recently was the one I have most personal ties with – Thunder Bay. Fort William and Port

Arthur, at the head of Lake Superior, had become Thunder Bay when the two cities amalgamated in 1970. It had taken me many visits to Canada before I went there. Having visited so many cities in Canada, I was astounded that you could go downtown with relatives and meet Lewis folk. On Sunday morning they arrived in church with my husband's books tucked under their arms to ask him about family connections. We had a wonderful gathering of Lewis folk arranged specially for our visit by Ian MacKenzie, Mayor of Portage la Prairie, and a grandson of Bàrd Chnoc Chùsbaig, author of songs like *Eilean Fraoich*. Everyone was encouraged to speak as much Gaelic as they could manage. One of the most memorable moments of the trip was when Ian took us to the grave of his grandfather.

Most of the Lewis people had gone out in the early decades of the twentieth century. Gaelic was their language but their sons and daughters were not encouraged to speak it. They understood a lot of the language but being in the city amongst many other cultures they did not speak it much. There were one or two who tried but found English a more comfortable language to express themselves in. Nan Anderson had lived in Sheshader in 1923 with her mother, sisters and grandparents. Her father had left for Canada to prepare a home for them and they left on the *Marloch* for Montreal later to join him.

Nan had a vivid memory of the emigrant ship the *Metagama* passing Sheshader with hundreds of young single men, one of them my Uncle George. She told me how they stood outside her grandfather's house and watched the great ship pass the village. The women were crying and she asked her mother why. Her mother said it was because the young men were leaving. Yet later Nan's mother left as well with her young children to join her husband. Nan told me in vivid detail of the trip to Glasgow and then to Montreal and on to Fort William, a journey of around 4,000 miles.

At the Emigration Conference I played a conversation I had with Bella MacDonald, *Bellag an Dotair*, from Branahuie, who married Captain Iain Tholstaidh MacDonald from Sheshader and who lives with him in Scarborough, Ontario. They were among those who emigrated to Canada in the 1960s, and Bella told me how she and Iain had visited a church in Loch Lomond, Cape Breton for a Gaelic service around 1970. The minister was from Thurso and he was an eighty-year-old man. They were piped in and out of the church and there were four precentors each taking turns to lay out a line of the psalm. They were told that this is what they did in Scotland in the past.

The people I have spoken about are only a very few of the Gaelic speakers I have met and recorded over twenty years of visits to Canada. It has been an inspiring experience and a privilege to go there and to collect the voices, stories and the songs of our own folk, so far from home, but who still have a great pride in the *seann dùthaich*, the old country, as they like to think of Scotland.

Notes

1. McDonnell, Sister Margaret. *The Emigrant Experience: Songs of Highland Emigrants in North America*, Toronto, 1982.
2. Business Plan, 2009 to 2010, Office of Gaelic Affairs, Nova Scotia.

7

ꕥ

Why Patagonia?

Greta Mackenzie

The emigration of Scottish people to Patagonia came in the wake of an earlier emigration of sheep-farm workers to the Falkland Isles in the South Atlantic. By the mid 1860s these islands were totally controlled by Britain and the Falkland Island Company (FIC) had established sheep-farms throughout the two main islands, East Falkland and West Falkland. They had offices in Liverpool from where they recruited workers throughout Britain, with a keen interest in attracting men from the Borders and the Highlands and Island areas of Scotland.

The Falkland Island Company were offering a free passage and accommodation and a reasonable wage with a pension after twenty years' service to men willing to emigrate to the Falklands to work as shepherds. The journey by sailing ship from Liverpool could take up to ninety days depending on weather conditions at sea. On arrival at Port Stanley, despite the company of compatriots and new friends made en route, the men could be in no doubt that they were now 8,000 miles away from home.

However, for the men arriving in the 1860s and 1870s the islands were in many ways a home from home as they bore a strong resemblance to the Outer Hebrides. They had the same combination of peat-bog, hill, moorland and pasture and an indented coastline with natural harbours and islets. The row of whitewashed cottages on the outskirts of Port Stanley was like a village inhabited by Scottish shepherds, some from the Inner and Outer Hebrides, from Inverness-shire, Ross-shire, Caithness and Sutherland, Perthshire, Dumfriesshire and Galloway. The weather also was similar to that back in Scotland, misty with frequent rain but with average sunshine and in winter heavy snowfalls.

Despite the strenuous work required of the men and the prolonged isolation from the rest of the world, life had its compensations. The simple, comfortable houses had their own poultry-run and kitchen garden for growing vegetables and potatoes. Outside there was a limitless supply of peat available for cutting for fuel, and on days of recreation the well-stocked rivers offered fish for anglers while for the hunting-minded there were geese, ducks and snipe a-plenty, as a welcome addition to the perennial diet of mutton, known among the islanders as '365'. Often they collected the eggs of penguins and wild geese.

Business flourished with the FIC but despite the rapid growth in the size of flocks there was an inevitable limit to the number of sheep that the islands' pastures could sustain. Settlements had been established in all corners of the main islands, and the few small islands that could be used also had their settlements. By the 1880s there was a serious risk of over-grazing. The economy of the islands was almost entirely dependent on sheep-farming and thereby at the mercy of the world price of wool. For shepherds who by now were aspiring to establish their own farms the outlook was becoming bleak as all the available land had been taken up by FIC, as were the top managerial posts.

News reached them that envious eyes on the rapid success of farming in the Falklands had prompted farmers in Britain, Spain and Germany to seek land in the southern regions of Patagonia. The governments in Argentina and Chile were offering huge tracts of land for mere pennies per acre for interested developers and already entrepreneurs were establishing settlements along the southern regions by the Straits of Magellan and in Tierra del Fuego. One such development was that of the company known as the 'Sociedad Esplotadora de Tierra del Fuego' established by a Spaniard by the name of Jose Menendez and a German by the name of Mauricio Braun, names that in later years became synonymous with the success and riches of sheep-farming.

Joining these first settlers were shepherds sailing the 300 miles from the Falklands, bringing with them sheep and dogs to the fertile Magellan fringe of Patagonia. The cost of the stock, brought across from the islands in quick schooners, varied at about a pound sterling per head, but the losses in transport, reaching almost 50 per cent, considerably increased the original figure. The first sheep imported were of the Lincoln and Merino breeds.

That immigration, of men skilled in every aspect of sheep-rearing, helped to lay the foundation for the expansion of large estancias throughout the huge territory of Patagonia. Some wanted to start up on their own while others were happy to take up employment with the already developing companies by the Straits of Magellan.

In Patagonia

Patagonia is an immense, sparsely populated region situated at the southern end of the South American continent shared between Argentina and Chile and taking in the island of Tierra del Fuego. Until the latter end of the nineteenth century it was largely unexplored, unmapped and uninhabited except for isolated settlements of native Indian tribes who had been there for thousands of years. Eastwards from the Andes to the Atlantic coast the seemingly endless, flat, dry and windswept plains are a treeless landscape with tussocks of grass separated from each other by gravel. For over a thousand miles it stretches, from north to south, with increasing monotony and aridity. Roaming across this vast area are herds of guanaco and the flightless, ostrich-like birds known as rheas.

Western Patagonia is a region of tremendous natural beauty and variety. The Andes mountains suddenly emerge as if out of nowhere, with spectacular glaciers feeding turquoise-blue lakes and fast-flowing rivers cascading into fertile valleys. Fjords and inlets cut into the continent and hundreds of densely forested islands lie offshore.

It was to this land that many hundreds of our island people made their way in search of employment on the fast-growing sheep-farms at the end of the nineteenth and the beginning of the twentieth centuries. Some were to find themselves tending many thousands of sheep deep inland on the pampa of Santa Cruz Province in Argentina, some in the Andean hills and valleys of Chile and others manning the slaughter-houses and freezing-plants (frigorificos) at various sites along the Straits of Magellan and in Tierra del Fuego. Indeed, some found employment on isolated islands further south in the Beagle Channel.

The earliest emigrants leaving the Outer Hebrides in the 1890s for Argentina and Chile arrived there at a time when the introduction of sheep to the land was causing much conflict with the native population of Indians. To the north of the Straits of Magellan lived the Tehuelche tribe who had roamed the pampa for generations living off the land, while across the Straits in Tierra del Fuego lived the Onas and the Yaghans, the latter tribe living off the islands in the Straits using small canoes to fish and gather shellfish and seaweed along the shores.

Each tribe had its own language and rich culture and to all of them sheep were hitherto unknown. They referred to them as 'white guanaco'. To them, the sheep now wandering over the land were fair game, just as were the guanaco and the rhea, and they saw no reason why they should not have a right to hunt them. They had little concept of the sheep belonging to someone else and in any case hunger now forced them to steal, as the guanaco, their staple food supply, was being forced further and further inland by the extensive fencing required by the farmers to protect their sheep.

The farmers complained bitterly of the marauding Indians cutting their fences and stealing hundreds and sometimes thousands of sheep at a time. Revenge was swift and guards were sent from the estancias to protect the flocks and the long stretches of boundary fencing. They carried guns and as they were directly answerable to their superiors for any losses, many Indians were shot in the course of duty and self-defence.

The early settlers had already introduced them to alcohol and diseases such as measles and influenza to which they had no immunity, and ultimately the Indians paid the price for the arrival of the avaricious European entrepreneurs. Within the space of three decades there were very few true Indians left in

Patagonia. In Punta Arenas cemetery a monument erected to 'The Unknown Indian' reads:

> *The unknown Indian came from the mists of history and geography. He lies here nestling in the bosom of his Chilean homeland. Eternally.*

My personal interest in this part of the world stems from my father Malcolm Smith of Cleascro, Achmore, and two of my uncles together with scores of their counterparts having been among the hundreds of people from the Western Isles to answer the call to Patagonia. Many of them, like my father, returned after a few years' sojourn in various parts of the region while others decided to remain there.

The estancia owners advertised for workers in newspapers throughout Scotland and recruiting agents were appointed in Inverness and Dumfries, in some cases the agent being the Church of Scotland minister of a parish. In the case of Lewis and Harris the agent was Rev. Donald MacCallum, residing in the manse at Keose, and indeed it was from the Lochs area of Lewis that the greatest number of men were recruited for shepherding. Possibly this was a clever move on the part of the sheep-farming owners as they thought that the minister in a parish would know his parishioners well and would recommend only physically fit, skilful and trustworthy men.

The emigrants to Patagonia made their way to Liverpool, their port of departure for South America, and the voyage, under sail, lasted for two months or more. By the late 1890s the faster passenger ships of The Pacific Steam Navigation Company had replaced the sailing ships and the voyage to Punta Arenas in the Straits of Magellan took around thirty days.

Representatives from the various estancias met the new recruit at the appropriate port of arrival in order to take him by horse and cart to the main farm, that could be two or three days' travel (and sometimes further) away.

Here he met the farm manager, was invited to rest for a day or two, and was given his instructions regarding the work of looking after several thousand sheep now in his care. He was provided with a troop of horses, sheepdogs (if he hadn't brought his own from home), a blanket and poncho for warmth, a gun and ammunition to deter predators such as puma and fox, and some provisions to last him for a month or so.

Another shepherd was assigned the task of accompanying the new arrival to his shanty very many miles away 'out on camp', which was to be his lonely abode from now on, some twenty or thirty miles distant from his nearest neighbour.

The shanty was usually a two-roomed shed of corrugated iron construction, with a wood-burning stove for heating and cooking, a table and chair, candles, a bed and a few cooking utensils. Once a month he would receive a delivery of provisions such as dried milk, dried beans, coffee, sugar, tea, flour and yeast to make his own bread. A good supply of firewood was essential, especially in the winter months when the night temperature often fell to more than twenty degrees below zero.

Outside there was a shelter for the horses and a kennel for the dogs. He had permission to kill a lamb or a sheep for meat for himself and the dogs and of course with his gun he could hunt for rabbits, hares, guanacos and ostrich to vary his diet of mutton.

In spring and summer, shearing and dipping times required the collective effort of all shepherds on the estancia and no doubt they looked forward to meeting together on such occasions for the exchange of news 'from home'. The entire wool-clip from some 30,000 or 40,000 sheep had to be sorted, weighed, pressed into bales and transported by horse-drawn wagons to the sea-port, a journey that required much preparation and planning and which took many days. Food and water for men and horses had to be carried, together with tents and cooking utensils for overnight camping en route.

The severity of the Patagonian winter added to the hardships of life on the pampa, with snowdrifts several feet deep lasting for weeks on end, taking a heavy toll on the sheep. The shepherd had to be 'on track' each day, digging out trapped sheep and moving them to safety. After a hard day's work, on arriving back at his shanty very cold, wet and hungry, he had to kindle his fire and prepare a hot meal. Often the kettle left bubbling on the red-hot stove before he retired to bed at night was, by morning, holding a block of ice!

My father often recalled one occasion when he had been caught out in a particularly bad blizzard some fifty miles out on camp on horseback. Night was falling with no sign of the blizzard easing off, and both horse and rider were nearing exhaustion. He dismounted and, seeing nowhere at all to offer shelter, it became quite evident to him that his life was now in danger. Having weighed up the situation, he knew that the action he must now take was a drastic one but necessary, if he was to save his own life. He shot his horse, disembowelled it and crept into its ribcage to seek shelter from the raging snowstorm and the severe cold.

The snow fell relentlessly during the next day and he spent a second night in his unconventional 'home' as the weather did not ease sufficiently for him to venture forth. By daybreak the sky had cleared and he started off on foot, and having trudged some distance he became aware of a lone rider heading in his direction. The Spaniard shepherd had spotted him and this kind man took him to his own shanty where he made my father comfortable and tended to him until he recovered.

I had heard other men tell how in similar circumstances of being caught out in severe weather, shepherds had suffered from hypothermia and frostbite, later resulting in the amputation of fingers and toes. We heard how some of our Islanders had lost their lives in snowstorms on these desolate and unforgiving plains.

Business Boom

Encouraged by the rapid and flourishing success of 'La Sociedad Esplotadora' many farmers from Britain and Europe arrived in Patagonia, some to join the company and others to establish businesses of their own. Recruitment of workers from England, Spain, France, Germany, Italy, Switzerland, Croatia and the Netherlands was brisk, and thousands of immigrants poured into the country in search of employment. Together with the Scottish settlers it was very much a multinational society, with the British in dominance. Wages were paid in sterling, building and engineering materials were imported from Britain, wool exportation was mainly to Britain and Europe, and a British Club and English School were established in Punta Arenas.

As well as shepherds and wool classifiers, labourers were recruited for fence-building, road-building and the building of bridges and dams; skilled workers were required for the construction of houses, abattoirs, freezing-plants, tallow-works; boat and barge-handlers were sought to facilitate the exportation of millions of tons of wool. As the years progressed and the big companies went from strength to strength, engineers were recruited for installation of telephone, electricity and water services, and with such growth of business there was requirement for office clerks, accountants and managers in the new banks that were springing up in the Southern territories.

Hotels and inns were erected in the remotest corners of distant parts and the hitherto barren wilderness was covered with innumerable flocks of thoroughbred sheep that rapidly made their owners very wealthy indeed, and helped to make Argentina the seventh wealthiest country in the world during that period.

Many of the men from the Western Isles who had started work as shepherds on the pampa progressed, through hard work, tenacity and a will to succeed, to become section managers or foremen on these large farms or found new employment within the companies, while others strived to buy or lease land and establish themselves in business. They seemed to have mastered the official Spanish language without much difficulty and I remember marvelling at how those who had returned from Patagonia could so effortlessly lapse into the language on meeting one another and reminiscing on past times in Patagonia.

I had heard the stories, I had listened to the Spanish being spoken around our own fireside and it was the curiosity aroused in me all those years ago that spurred me on to 'go see for myself'.

And so it was that in 1994, in 1996 and again in 2002, some members of my family and myself made our way to Patagonia in the hope that we could learn more about this fascinating land and the life of the island emigrants who made it their destination over a hundred years ago. We wondered if we would meet any descendants of the emigrants who had chosen to live out their lives there, but as there had been little contact for fifty years or more, perhaps it was too much to expect.

Descendants in Buenos Aires

Buenos Aires was our first stop on each of our trips to South America, as indeed it had been for many of these early travellers to Patagonia. Here, many of them had taken their first steps on foreign soil and how different a world it must have seemed to them with its thronging crowds, its Spanish language and its multinational population. We surmised that here perhaps could be found descendants living in retirement from the southern regions of Argentina. Given the enormous size of this city and with the short time at our disposal, it became obvious that our task was not easy.

Some weeks prior to our departure I had heard Kenny MacIver of our local radio station interviewing a gentleman by the name of Guillermo Santana Mackinley talking from Buenos Aires. So impressed was I by his knowledge and fluency of Gaelic that I had to enquire who he was. Kenny was happy to give me Guillermo's contact details and I decided to write to him asking if it would be possible to meet him when we were in Buenos Aires. This was the start of a friendship with the Mackinley family that lasts to this day.

Guillermo is a descendant of a Scottish family who arrived in Argentina in the middle years of the nineteenth century. He was born in Buenos Aires some fifty years ago and throughout his life he has had a great love for Scotland and everything Scottish, including the Gaelic language. His wife Patsy shares his enthusiasm and they have established the Gaelic choir of Buenos Aires and the Gaelic School that Guillermo runs for learners of the language once or twice a week in the capital.

We were invited to visit them in their home on the outskirts of the city and some of their friends were there to meet us too. One of the ladies present was Beatrice de Zapata, who had fluent English and was excitedly telling me that her late father was Scottish and that she had been brought up in Southern Patagonia but had never seen Scotland. She produced an album of photographs and the first one she showed me was of the home her father left in 1907. I was speechless! The picture was of the house that was still standing and of nearby ruins by the shore, only a stone's throw away from my own home in the village of Keose. 'Are you the daughter of Donald Maciver?' I asked, much to her surprise. That in this city of over 13 million population I had met a Keose descendant within twelve hours of arriving was quite unbelievable! Beatrice and her brother Hugh Maciver later paid a visit to Lewis, in 1999, and were able to meet with their relatives on the island.

It was equally hard to believe that on the following morning we found a second descendant! We had visited St. Andrew's Presbyterian Church in the city and after the service we were invited to have a cup of tea in the vestry. While chatting I showed some photos that my father had brought from Patagonia and a young lady called out, 'That is my grandfather!' I had found a member of the Bain family, for whom my father and uncle had worked as shepherds on their estancias for several years, in Santa Cruz province.

The family of five brothers had emigrated from Lybster around 1899 and had established their own farm some distance from Puerto Deseado. Ingrid Bain invited us to her parents' home that evening and we were able to catch up with several members of the Bain family, hear the history of their pioneering years in Patagonia and their recollection of Lewis workers on the farms. One of the farms mentioned in conversation was 'Estancia Caledonia' that was managed by Malcolm Macdonald of Carloway, Lewis, father of Alex Macdonald, presently Convenor of Western Isles Council. In fact Alex spent the first few years of his childhood on the estancia before his parents decided to return to Lewis.

Members of the Bain family have been to visit their relatives in Caithness in the past few years. Alex Macdonald, along with members of his family, has been back to visit his birthplace and also the Bain family in Argentina.

On our last visit to Buenos Aires in 2002 we had the pleasure of meeting Elizabeth Morrison, daughter of Kenneth Morrison of Airidhbhruaich who emigrated to Patagonia in 1914, and also Sarah Macdonald, daughter of John Macdonald who had left Keose in 1910. Sadly both Elizabeth Morrison and Sarah Macdonald have since passed away. Also on that visit we met a descendant of one of the earliest emigrants from Lewis, Angus Martin of Balallan, who arrived in Punta Arenas in 1893.

Descendants in Rio Gallegos

Flying south from Buenos Aires to Rio Gallegos for 1,500 miles we noted on the map the names we had heard in our younger days: Commodoria Rivadavia, Bahia Blanca, Chubut, Puerto Santa Cruz, San Julian, all of which were familiar places to Islanders. Looking from the air over the flat expanse below, it was obvious to us that we were about to set foot on the pampa proper, that wind-blown land where if trees grow at all, they grow upwards for a couple of feet and then parallel with the ground.

On arrival in the city we had a chance meeting with an English-speaking lady. We remarked on her knowledge of

English, and she answered, 'Of course I speak English, I am a Mackenzie from Scotland'. She introduced herself as Mayo Mackenzie, whose grandfather, William Mackenzie, had left the Helmsdale district in the early 1900s and had settled in this area and had owned 'Estancia Coy Inlet', now run by Mayo and her husband John Hewlitt. Did Mayo know of any other Scottish descendants? She pointed down the street and said that Alejandro Mackenzie living close by was of Hebridean descent. We knocked on his door and unfortunately he was not at home but a neighbour appeared from next door and we understood from her that Alejandro and his wife were presently out on their farm.

The 'Museo de Pioneros' looked interesting so we stepped in to have a look. Portraits gazed at us from the walls, many of them of Scots people who had left their mark on the great sheep-farming period in Argentina. The Tehuelche and Ona native Indian period was well presented, reminding us that our father had actually befriended some of these people in the early 1920s. It had been a lady of the Tehuelche tribe who had sewn the guanaco-skin bedcovers that had kept us warm as children growing up in Achmore. Father had brought them on his return from Puerto Deseado in 1927. The exhibits within the museum were very British in character, testimony to the superiority of that community within Patagonia for some thirty years or more.

The following morning we were on our way by bus to Punta Arenas, 180 miles distant, and when we arrived at passport control on the Chilean border it was a relief to escape the dusty confines of the bus and breathe fresh air again. A tall, lean gentleman with a weather-beaten face stood on the pavement as we emerged and, stepping forward, he asked if there were any British people on the bus. Imagine our surprise when he introduced himself and his wife as Alejandro and Jessie Mackenzie! Their neighbour had phoned them at their farm to say visitors had tried to contact them the previous day and that they were to be travelling on the daily bus to Punta Arenas on the following day.

Alejandro was the son of Hector and Dolina Mackenzie from Airidhbhruaich in Lewis, who had arrived in Rio Gallegos in the early years of 1903. They settled there and Alejandro, one of a large family, had followed in his father's footsteps, eventually becoming a partner in a large company owning the 'Estancia Monte Aymond' on the border of Argentina and Chile. He married Jessie Urquhart, whose parents had emigrated from Ullapool, and they have one daughter, Gem. We were very happy on our return to Lewis to convey the news of them to their cousins in Airidhbhruaich and delighted that the Mackenzies travelled from Argentina to Lewis a few years later.

On subsequent visits to Rio Gallegos we received a wonderful welcome in their home and Gem was our guide and interpreter in 2002 when we crossed the pampa to visit the Patagonian Ice Cap. Again, I am sad to report that Alejandro passed away in 2006.

While on that long and monotonous bus journey to Punta Arenas from Rio Gallegos I could not but think of the pioneers who covered the same distance on horseback, sometimes driving flocks of hundreds or even thousands of sheep.

In Rio Gallegos we met members of the family of Angus Martin of Balallan who had arrived there in 1893. Having worked on various farms along the Straits, buying and selling sheep as he went along, Angus eventually reached Rio Gallegos, where he found employment with the 'Company of Curtze, Walen, Williams and Suarez', stocking the land known as 'Las Horquetas'.

He worked faithfully for twelve years, winning the esteem of his employers and of all the settlers of that time. For a period of time, while carrying out the tasks required of him, he lived in a very remote area in his tiny shelter consisting of six sheets of zinc, enduring temperatures of twenty degrees below zero and living on hard tack biscuits, dried beans, mutton and, perhaps, game brought down by his own gun.

When his work at 'Las Horquetas' ended he moved to the area of 'Chank Aike', which he stocked for another important firm in the area. In 1907, determined to work for his own account, he followed the course of the River Gallegos, often guided by Tehuelche Indians who were knowledgeable of the land and of the safe fords on the river. He pitched his tent on the land that is the property of the Martin family to this present time. By the year 1919 he had married and had established the well-known 'Estancia Chali Aike', now managed by his great grandson Gonzalo and family. Sonia Martin, a great granddaughter, lives in El Calafate, where we met up with her and her husband.

Some members of the Martin family have visited Lewis to meet their new-found relatives, while Lewis cousins have made the trip to Buenos Aires and Rio Gallegos. As with the families of many of the people who had decided to remain in Patagonia, contact had been lost over the last fifty or sixty years of the twentieth century and it is very gratifying to see the relatives now reunited.

I had heard of a friend and neighbour of Angus Martin who had also emigrated in these early years and remained there. He was John Montgomery from Balallan who, through the same strong will and determination to succeed in business for himself, established his own farm in Chile and became renowned in the region as a prize-winning breeder of Merino sheep and also of cattle. We had the pleasure of meeting his daughter, Peggy Montgomery, in Santiago in 2002 and she also has been to Lewis to visit her relatives here.

In Puerto Natales, north of Punta Arenas, we enquired of people in our hotel if they knew of any descendants of Kenneth Morrison, Kyles Scalpay, who had owned 'Estancia Maria Sofia'. We were told that his daughter, Susannah, was living close by, and we called in to say 'hello' and bring greetings from her cousin Donald John Morrison of Kyles Scalpay. She was very happy to see folk from her father's native homeland.

Descendants in Punta Arenas

As our bus pulled into the terminal in Punta Arenas late of a summer's evening in February 1994, there was no mistaking the very Hebridean face of Peggy Mackay who stood among the group of people waiting outside. She knew of our intended arrival and she gave us a cheerful Gaelic greeting '*Failte oirbh gu Punta Arenas*', adding that this was the first opportunity that she had had in her lifetime of welcoming visitors from her father's native village of Achmore.

Peggy's father, Malcolm Mackay, had begun work as a shepherd on the 'Cerro Guido' section of one of the large farms by the Straits of Magellan in 1907 and after seven years he returned to Lewis to marry the girl who had been waiting for him all that time – Christina Macdonald – from the village of Leurbost. Together they headed back to Patagonia in 1917 to his new job as manager of one of the big farms by the Straits of Magellan. Here they raised a family of four, Peggy, Aulay, Chrissie and Allan.

For many of the Scottish families living in remote estancias, education of the children became a problem when they reached school age. It was usual for the families to return to Lewis for the purpose of enrolling the child in the school of the parents' native village, if there were grandparents or other relatives residing there who were willing to be the child's (or children's) guardians. It often proved too expensive to have several children living in lodgings in Punta Arenas during term-time while attending school there. Chrissie and Allan were taken to their aunt's home in Lewis and were enrolled in Achmore school, while Peggy and Aulay remained in Punta Arenas.

On reaching retirement age Malcolm and Christina decided to return to their native Lewis and set up home in Achmore. Peggy Mackay married John Fell, grandson of one of the original Scottish pioneers in Patagonia who had established 'Estancia Brazo Norte', 180 miles north of Punta Arenas. John had inherited the farm and after his death Peggy continued to run 'Estancia Brazo Norte' with the help of her son Johnnie. Now in retirement she has sold the farm and she resides in the city of Punta Arenas.

When visiting Punta Arenas in 1996, we were invited to share a very special occasion being celebrated by the Mackay family. Allan and Chrissie had returned to the city to spend a holiday with Peggy and Aulay. It was the first time that the family had been together in their place of birth in the space of sixty-five years!

On our first day in the city we noticed a red truck with the name Donald Macleod emblazoned on its side. Peggy explained that it belongs to the grandson of Donald Macleod of Balallan, another of the early emigrants who established his own business, and we had the pleasure of meeting

Donnie Macleod's father and his Croatian wife Angelita on a subsequent visit in 2002. They were able to tell us the history of the early founding of the 'Sociedad Esplotadora de Tierra del Fuego' and of the enormous contribution made by the Highland and Island emigrants to its success throughout Patagonia.

A big surprise awaited us in Punta Arenas on our very first visit! We had visited the large city cemetery to look for the grave of Donald Smith, a first cousin of my father, who had left from Keose, Lewis in 1910 and who had married a lady of French descent and settled there. Eventually, with the help of the very obliging office staff, we did discover it and noted that Donald had passed away in 1963. Alongside were the graves of Josephina, his wife, and that of two sons named Donald and Guillermo. Two days later, on returning from a trip to the Torres del Paine National Park, as we stepped off the bus we were astonished to see two people walking in our direction, hands outstretched in greeting. The tall gentleman introduced himself as Angus Roderick Smith and with him was his sister Isabel – the two surviving members of the family of Donald Smith and Josephina Yung. We had found relatives in Punta Arenas of whom we had no previous knowledge! That same evening we had the pleasure of meeting their extended families, and a close friendship with them all has ensued. Several members of the Smith family in Punta Arenas have since visited us in Lewis and have met their many relations here on the island and elsewhere in Scotland.

Our all-too-short stay in Punta Arenas was over and it was time to cross the Straits of Magellan to Tierra del Fuego.

Descendants in Tierra del Fuego

'Estancia Jose Menendez', in the capital Rio Grande, was our next stop, to visit Angus Smith, who had managed the farm for a period of forty years. His father and mother had emigrated from Achmore, Lewis to Patagonia and settled on 'Estancia Anita' in Argentina, again owned by Menendez. After the death of his parents, Angus went to Rio Grande and in 1996, when we first met him, he was considering retirement.

He had seen many changes occurring in the fortunes of the sheep-farming business during these decades, but the farm still supports many thousands of sheep and also a large number of cattle. The greatest change over the past decade is that Rio Grande is now the destination for anglers from all over the world to sample the excellent sea-trout fishing during the summer months, the imposing farmhouse now acting as their fishing lodge for the duration of their stay.

It was interesting that Angus retained the Gaelic language of his parents and was very fluent in it, as of course he was in Spanish, but struggled a bit when he spoke in English. We greatly enjoyed our visit to Rio Grande and we were happy to see Angus when he paid a visit to Lewis in 1998, catching up with his relatives in Achmore and Carloway. Sadly, by the time we visited Rio Grande again in 2002, Angus had passed away some months previously and he is greatly missed by his many friends there.

Across on the Chilean sector of Tierra del Fuego we spent an unforgettable week on a farm where another Lewis descendant had spent many years of her life. Mary Morrison was the daughter of Kenneth Morrison who had made his way from Boghaglas in Harris and had spent many years living with his wife and daughter on Dawson Island in the Straits of Magellan, where he had established his own farm. Mary married Gaston Fuentes, owner of 'Estancia La Frontera', and they had one daughter, also called Mary. We had met Mary when she visited her relatives in Harris and Lewis in the mid 1990s and again with her father when we were in Punta Arenas in 2002. Gaston Fuentes and Mary kindly offered us the use of their home on 'La Frontera' as they were to be away for a week, and it was very exciting to sample life for ourselves on an estancia in Patagonia!

On our way there, we stopped in Porvenir to say 'hello' to Kitty Morrison, daughter of Neil Morrison from Uig and Mary Montgomery from Habost, Lochs, who also were among the emigrants of the early 1900s. Kitty has three sons living in Punta Arenas.

Before leaving the Straits of Magellan we wanted to pay a visit to Kenneth Maclean and his family living on 'Estancia El Trebol' on Isla Riesco. Kenneth was the son of Peter W. Maclean from Crowlista, Uig, who was well known to all the early settlers in Punta Arenas as manager of a bank there and also as a popular piper at weddings and social occasions in the city. His son Kenneth was renowned throughout Patagonia as a judge at shows of Merino and Corriedale breeds and he himself has been the recipient of many such prizes throughout his farming career. Sadly, since our enjoyable visit to their hospitable home in 2002, Kenneth has passed away. 'Estancia El Trebol' continues to be managed by his son Roderick.

A neighbouring farm on Isla Riesco, 'Estancia Dinah', is owned by a member of the Macleay family from Shieldaig who has a relative, Murdo Livingstone, living in Stornoway. Murdo has recently told me that nine family members of the Macleays visited the site of their ancestors in Shieldaig and Applecross in 2009.

It is gratifying indeed that the 'home-coming' is on-going and I am very happy to say that over the past few years we have had visits from twenty people from this distant part of the world keen to see the land from which their grandparents and great grandparents left. Equally, I am pleased to say that several people known to us have made the journey from the Outer Hebrides to Patagonia to meet with long-lost relatives there.

8

ᘓ

Emigrant Experiences

Chris McIntyre, Norman MacRae and Annie MacRitchie

The conference included a session chaired by Kenny MacIver of BBC Radio nan Gaidheal at which returning emigrants or people with overseas and island connections talked about their experiences. Among those participating were Tully McIntyre of Seattle, USA, whose ancestors were from Benbecula and who was visiting the Outer Hebrides along with his wife Chris for the first time; Norman MacRae, who was born in Detroit, USA of Lewis emigrant parents who returned with their family to Lewis in 1947 when Norman was six years old; and Annie MacRitchie, who emigrated to Detroit from Lewis in 1952 at the age of twenty-three and was visiting her homeland at the time of the conference.

Tully McIntyre spoke with emotion about the warm welcome he and his wife had received in the islands, and how he felt a close link with the people even though this was his first visit. He and Chris had been on an archaeological dig in South Uist immediately prior to the conference, and Chris has written a summary of their experiences there, which is reproduced with her kind permission below.

Chris McIntyre

We had fun recently in digging up history, both Scotland's and our own! Reading through *Earthwatch*, an archaeological magazine, I saw an advertisement for a trip to Scotland's South Uist. It is one of the Outer Hebrides islands just west of the Isle of Skye. The article called it a 'treeless island with white sand beaches'. This place is in our family genealogy and I thought we had to go. Even though we had never been on an archaeological dig, this was the ground my husband Tully's ancestors lived on. We spent three weeks in Scotland, two on the dig, and one sight-seeing (which was not enough). We flew to Glasgow and then took a very small plane to South Uist.

The sun was brilliant in the blue sky as we descended over South Uist into the airport on Benbecula. These are two of the islands in the Outer Hebrides. All we could see from the air were ponds (lochs), inlets and outlets creating a mosaic with the land of Tully's forefathers. His great-great-grandparents lived on Benbecula, were married in South Uist, and eventually emigrated from the port of Lochboisdale to Canada during the time of the Clearances. The islands looked very rugged, almost desolate, as we approached. We disembarked, armed with mason trowels, raingear, kneepads, boots, warm clothing and some trepidation about taking on this task with a bunch of college students half our age.

We were met at the airport by three Cockney Brits and a leader from Sheffield University, sponsor of the dig. We were part of a volunteer force. We were shuttled down to Gearraidh Bhailteas in South Uist near the Flora MacDonald site and the Milton House, which served as the operative center for the expedition. We were dispersed among three cottages and settled in to get acquainted with our roommates, hosts and the surrounding countryside that was our home for the next two weeks. We had a vegetarian diet and peat fires! Is this what is meant by going back to the land? We walked, within a mile or so, across the machair (flat grassy plain) and discovered the incredible beauty of the Outer Hebrides. The mountains behind us to the east, the lush green pastures with their wildflowers, and the white sand beaches as far as you can see as we reached the Atlantic Ocean. We walked and sat for a couple of hours as we gazed at a sunset as resplendent as any we have ever seen. If it were twenty or so degrees warmer, you would think you were somewhere in the South Seas. We didn't see another person the entire time we were on the beach.

Walking to the dig site the first morning we had no idea what the next two weeks held for us as this was our first archaeological expedition. We arrived three weeks into the project which included nine partially dug trenches 3 feet by 40 feet. It had a large garden area containing a rock constructed corn drier which had been buried for several decades. We were surrounded by testimony to the hardy, rugged subsistence lives our forefathers led – old farm equipment, fishing nets and floats, lobster pots, and rudimentary gardening hand tools. We were watched over by the roaming cows, chickens and sheep among the wildflowers and fresh Atlantic Ocean air.

I will never look at the soil, rolling pastures, or sandy shores again without wondering what secrets are held in the humps and valleys that are no longer just nature's deposits. These might be foundations, pathways of past lives, toils and travels, or final resting places of rock constructed burial cairns. The archaeological crew taught us to remove the soil with the edge of our trowels one small layer at a time. Thousands of scraping motions yielded bits of history in the form of pottery pieces, spear and lance points, coins, earthen samples of ash and midden, and one wax seal from a liquor bottle dating to the 1700s. I unearthed three degraded iron pieces which seemed odd to me. One of the Boston University archaeological students studied the pieces for about thirty seconds and proceeded to let out a whoop and cry as she fitted the segments together. She held up a spear or arrow point which dated our trench to the fourteenth century according to Jim Symonds, our director from Sheffield University. As the trenches were unfolded we charted, plotted, took photographs, and catalogued hundreds of specimens.

We found ourselves visualising our ancestors living on these very soils, performing their tasks for simple survival. We toured the islands of South Uist and Benbecula filled with so much history. There were ruins of ancient castles, blackhouses, burial cairns (one dating back 4,000 to 5,000 years) and circular, excavated areas a hundred yards across with standing stones placed strategically at the perimeter. Gaining some insight into their lives, with the elements, as they worked the crofts and supported the various townships was a fascinating journey. We visited St. Michael's Church in South Uist where Tully's great-great-grandparents were married in 1825. We reviewed the actual church records of the marriage and subsequent baptism of their firstborn. Everyone we talked to seem to guide us to someone else or another source of information as we searched for our roots of the McIntyre Clan. We made friends and acquaintances wherever we went. We can hardly wait to return 'home' to all the warm, helpful, interesting and enjoyable people that welcomed us and made our trip one of the most enriching experiences of our lives.

Norman MacRae

Growing up in Detroit, USA

I suppose the story should start back in 1923. My father, Angus MacRae (probably better known as 'Scotch', although maybe not at that time), was an eighteen-year-old working as a farm labourer at Goathill Farm on the outskirts of Stornoway. As far as I can ascertain now, he had been working there since he left school at fourteen. At the relatively tender age of eighteen he applied and was accepted for emigration to Canada where he was to work on a farm. He set sail on the *Metagama* on Saturday 21 April, 1923. There were another twenty-eight men and women from the Back area making the same journey. On arrival in Canada he worked for some time on a farm but was able to cross over into the States to visit friends and relatives whenever he could. On one of these visits he failed to return to Canada and thereafter settled in Detroit, Michigan (illegal immigration seemed to have been commonplace even then). He was soon able to get a job at the Ford car plant as a security guard. He was one of the fortunate few who had work right through the Depression and eventually became a naturalised US Citizen.

My mother, Isabella Macarthur from Carloway, emigrated to the States in 1929. She had worked at 'the fishing', mostly along the East Coast from Yarmouth to Lerwick, and on arrival in Detroit found work as a housekeeper. There were numerous island girls there, some from Carloway she knew well and others she very soon got to know from Back. She became life-long friends in particular with Dolag Bheag and Ciorstiona Mhuillear.

The Lewis Society was in its heyday at that time and of course all the young folk from the island attended the dances and other social gatherings. It was at one of these she espied Scotch across the dancefloor. It was love at first sight as far as she was concerned and she determined in that moment he was the man for her. Apparently he had a girlfriend at the time but that did not deter her and they were married on 10 June 1933. I never found out who the poor girl was who got elbowed aside.

My recollections of life in Detroit are still pretty vivid. My mother used to relate a story that when I was only weeks old my brother Angie, who was four years my senior, lifted me out of my cot to show me off to a neighbour, a Mr Ploshnic who was passing in the street. We stayed in a house one up and Angie was leaning over the balcony with me in his arms. It was the shouting of the neighbour, 'No Angie, I don't want to see your baby', that attracted my mother's attention and she came to the rescue.

While the war was ongoing, there were no real shortages that I was aware of. We had all the mod cons that were available and a car, a pretty old and battered black Ford. We used to go to a house on lakes upstate for our holidays, memories of which still linger. An annual picnic was held by Members of the Lewis Society on an island called Boblo situated in the Windsor River bordering the States and Canada. It was a huge event with plenty food, piping and dancing and of course plenty to keep the kids occupied. This event was certainly celebrated up until recent years by second and third generations of Leòdhasachs but the venue changed to Grosse Pointe on the mainland. I'm not sure whether it is still ongoing or not.

I remember one day being with Angie and a few others and entering the door of a building a couple of streets away. We all had a sip of water from a container at the door little realising that the building was a chapel and the water was holy water to be used by worshippers as they entered. No wonder it tasted awful.

On another occasion I was with the boy downstairs, who was about my own age, playing in the back alley. His parents had a cafeteria and somehow or other he had managed to get a hold of some cigarettes from the cafe. The two of us started puffing away and soon it seemed not such a good idea. I began to feel sick and ran home with my head spinning. My father was on family duty that day as my mother was working. He thought I was suffering from sun-stroke. He phoned the doctor and related the symptoms. The doctor asked him, 'Has he been smoking?' My father said, 'He is only three.' The doctor replied, 'Go and ask him.' Under interrogation I cracked and admitted everything. I must have retained memories of my father's interrogation methods which came in handy in my later life.

Life in the States came to a conclusion on 18 September 1947, when the family returned home to Lewis and to the croft at 46 Vatisker. I still recollect vaguely being on the *Queen Elizabeth* during the crossing and docking at Southampton where the sight of a policeman standing on the dock wearing a strange helmet seemed very odd indeed.

I was six years of age when we arrived at 46 and had never seen a cow or sheep before, and efforts to ride them met with utter failure. Life had suddenly become very different from what we had been used to. My father's parents were both living then but my grandmother died six weeks after we arrived. It is alleged – and I have no reason to cast doubt on the story – that when Granny died and it came to the day of the funeral the coffin was placed in the back of the bus to be taken to the cemetery – there was no such thing as a hearse in those days, certainly not in Back. When the bus returned from the cemetery either Angie or I was heard to say, 'that's the bus back but Granny isn't on it'. I don't know what we had expected.

With no electricity, running water or inside toilet facilities it was indeed a change of lifestyle. The toilet was the byre, which was across the road, and with only a torch to show the way, care had to be exercised that the cow didn't answer a call of nature at the same time. We frequently tried to teach the cat to swim in the cask filled with rainwater from the roof but it never really got the hang of it.

Of course we were unable to speak Gaelic at the time and I can't remember being conscious that it caused difficulties in play or subsequently when we were able to converse fluently in the language. It just seemed to happen.

I started school in the ABC class, as it was known, with Katag Mhurchaidh the teacher. I can't remember that being a particularly joyful experience but matters improved out of all measure when we passed onto the next class with Mrs Stewart, Banntrach na Pòcaid. She frequently used to throw us sweets from her own desk. No wonder she was very popular. How she managed it with rationing still ongoing I don't know.

I think it is time to draw this to a close, but before I do I would just like to say that there were three children in our family. My late sister Ishbel was thirteen (obviously a bit older and much wiser) when we came back to Lewis. She went directly to the Nicolson Institute and from there on to Skerries College in Glasgow to do Secretarial Studies. She married and remained in Glasgow till her sudden death at the age of thirty-six.

Annie MacRitchie

Reminiscences

On 19 October 2009, the day before she left Stornoway to return to Detroit, Annie MacRitchie was interviewed by Marjory Harper on the telephone. During the hour-long conversation she enlarged on issues she had mentioned during the interview panel at the conference five weeks earlier. Her experiences of emigration and settlement are summarised below:

In December 1952, twenty-three-year-old Annie Matheson left her native Isle of Lewis for a new life in Detroit. After more than five decades in the city where she settled, married and raised four children, she still thinks of Lewis as 'home' and since 1994 she has returned to the island for a month each year.

Annie's story is a familiar one. While growing up in the village of Coll she had heard much about the United States from neighbours whose sons, daughters and siblings had emigrated, and she was so fascinated by their stories that she decided to follow in their footsteps as soon as possible. She contrasted her job in a Stornoway clothing store – where after eight years her starting wage of 30 shillings a week had risen to £3 10s – with the untold riches of the USA, where the perception was that earnings were 'ten times that much'. Post-war blues in ration-blighted Britain reinforced her decision to secure a sponsor and apply for a visa.[1]

Annie's emigration was triggered not only by a quest for escape, adventure and betterment, coupled with the knowledge that she was following a well-trodden route: affairs of the heart played a part as well, for her husband-to-be (Norman

MacRitchie) had emigrated from Coll about a year earlier and, like many other Lewismen, had found a job on the Great Lakes. Although Annie had dreaded telling her parents that she was leaving, anticipating that 'my mother especially would be maybe angry', she found that they were 'quite reconciled, and they didn't put any stumbling blocks in my way'. Her departure and subsequent experiences were followed with interest not only by her family but also within the local community, where many could still recall the sailing of the iconic *Metagama* almost thirty years earlier.[2] 'When I left for the States', she recalled, 'I think I called at every house in the neighbourhood where I lived to say goodbye because I knew them all so well.... We had a lot of relatives and neighbours and friends, they would all be interested. For it was a big thing, one from the community, going, doing what I did. They would all ask my parents – "well, have you heard yet, how she got on?"'

After shipping her steamer trunk ahead to Southampton, Annie took the mail and passenger boat *Loch Ness* from Stornoway to Mallaig, via Kyle of Lochalsh. She continued by train to Glasgow, where she stayed for a couple of days before proceeding to London for the weekend. 'At that time ... there was terrible smog in London and I remember when we went out of the place where I was staying we had to have these cotton neckerchiefs around our neck and nose because the soot was just flying in the air and a lot of people had died from chest ailments due to that smog.' Delivered to Southampton by the Monday morning boat train, she boarded the *Queen Elizabeth* for a five-day voyage that on Saturday morning saw her disembark in New York. The experience, she recalls, was pleasurable, the inevitable seasickness notwithstanding.

> *It was just like being in a floating luxury hotel. You had your own waiter at the table, you were assigned a table and you had your own waiter, white linen cloths and big linen napkins and huge fruit – oranges and apples that you never saw in your life. And you got excellent meals. Printed menu, I still have some of these menus that I saved … I shared my cabin with two or three war brides who were going across and another older woman, and it was interesting to talk to them.… The first two days were fine and the last two, but in between I was very seasick. Even though the boat was big it was stormy in the winter time and … I think I was lying low for two or three days.*[3]

Accompanied by her fiancé, who had travelled to New York and was waiting on the pier to meet the boat, Annie caught the train straight to Detroit, 'a beautiful city, it was just like being in another world … very clean, a lot of things going on, a lot of traffic, more cars than I ever had imagined'. Until the Christmas holidays were over she stayed with her sponsor, a distant relative, but she had no difficulty in securing a job, the economy being 'probably at a peak when I went out there'. On 2nd January she started work with the Chapin family, looking after their four young children and performing other household duties as required. Her board and lodging were provided, as well as a handsome wage, and during the year that she worked for the Chapins – whose wealth derived from the automobile industry – she was able to save enough money for her forthcoming wedding. She was also given an invaluable induction into American habits and customs, punctuated by occasional encounters with well-known figures on the international stage.

> *It was a wonderful experience when I lived with an American family. I got used to the American cooking, the food they ate was different, and the way they served, you know, the servings, the way they set a table and all that. It was an opportunity for me to learn these things. It would have been harder if I wasn't living with an American family, to get into the way of life. So I was very happy to be there. And although they were very wealthy people they were so nice, they just treated me like I was one of themselves.... [Roy Chapin's] father founded the Hudson Motor Car Company and then they joined with Studebaker Parker while I was working with them and they formed American Motors.... They used to have Henry Ford at his home – I met him and his wife. They were there for dinner and I waited table and I thought she was like a china doll. I never saw a real person as dainty looking as she was. She was just immaculate and just like a painted doll.... I met the ambassador to Belgium who was a guest at their house too.*[4]

The transatlantic gulf in living standards was particularly evident in the 1950s. Annie felt that she was 'just living in luxury compared with conditions in post-war Britain, and the wages were so much higher in America. You could go to the store and buy care packages to send to Britain, you could buy butter in tins and sugar packaged specially for that purpose ... I did it a few times.' Having completed his first season on the Great Lakes, Norman MacRitchie was able to buy a car and five years after their marriage the family, which by then included two children, was able to pay the first of two three-month winter visits back to Lewis. In later years, when the nine-month absences from the family that accompanied the lake work were exchanged for the greater stability of home-based employment with the Ford Motor Company, the MacRitchies travelled regularly to different parts of the United States and Canada, as well as making several six-week summer sojourns to Lewis.

Particularly in the early years, Annie's life was rooted in the Lewis community of Detroit. When she arrived in that city of one million inhabitants, 'there were several hundred Lewis people working there', 90 per cent of them with General Motors, Chrysler and Ford. In the locality where her sponsor lived she could count about twenty households whose extended families she knew in Lewis and who offered her hospitality and friendship. As a result, she never felt homesick. Within a year she had also been followed to Detroit by two friends with whom she had worked in Stornoway, one of whom responded to a wealthy family's advertisement offering to sponsor a live-in children's nanny, while the other also lived with her sponsor, but took up office work. Linguistic identity was also preserved, although the MacRitchies, like many of their contemporaries, deliberately avoided teaching Gaelic to their children. 'I felt that it was better to use English for their education, I felt, well, the Gaelic isn't going to help them that much, I'd rather them be fluent in English than have a mixture.'[5] The Lewis Society of Detroit, established in 1919, provided a formal mechanism for social and charitable support, at least to the inter-war wave of migrants who had to struggle with the impact of the Depression. In the post-war generation, however, the Society struggled, a malaise that Annie attributes to better conditions in Britain having stemmed the flow of Hebridean emigrants.

The institution that has been of greatest and most enduring influence in Annie's life, however, is the Detroit congregation of the Free Church of Scotland, which has provided spiritual support, social networks and a tangible link with her homeland.

Her husband's older brother, Murdo MacRitchie, had just been called as minister to the Detroit congregation in 1952, after completing postgraduate studies at Westminster Theological Seminary in Philadelphia, and by the time Annie arrived a building had been constructed.[6]

> *The church that I belonged to in Lewis, they opened a church in Detroit and that kept, I think, a lot of the Lewis people together. You know, the church was a centre where we all met and worshipped and they were very, very wonderful people. They helped each other out, they were very close to each other.*

When Murdo MacRitchie was called to a charge in Stornoway in the 1960s the Detroit congregation entered upon a thirty-year period during which there was no settled ministry, but when Free Church practices were maintained by visiting clergy seconded from Scotland, usually for six-month sojourns. Although Gaelic services have long ceased to be held, and Annie is one of only a small remnant of Hebridean-born members in a largely American congregation, the church has retained exclusive, unaccompanied psalm singing and the authorised version of the Bible. Now the only surviving Free Church congregation in the USA[7] – although in the 1970s it dropped the suffix 'of Scotland' from its name in an effort to dismantle cultural barriers – it has in recent years had a permanent minister in the person of Lewis-born Kenny D. Macleod.

The most personal transatlantic links were maintained through correspondence, visits and – later – telephone calls. Although Annie's parents never came to see her in Detroit, both her sisters visited several times. Annie was a faithful correspondent who also eagerly anticipated the receipt of news from home:

> *Every day I wrote and every day I got plenty mail from my parents, my sister, my sisters and brother – all my relatives and all my friends. Every day it was, my treat was looking forward to the mail man.... Letter writing is a thing of the past. I myself write, I always wrote, but the last few years it's the phone, I use the phone, because the phone rates are more reasonable now than they were.... When I went to the States nobody here had telephones except businesses. Private homes, hardly anybody I knew had telephones in their homes. ... I've saved letters over the years from special people, and I'm glad I did because I have boxes of them and I go through them – when I've nothing better to do I do that, I read the letters from way, from years and years ago, from the fifties when I came over here first.*

When asked to offer some concluding reflections on more than half a century of life in the United States, Annie acknowledged the huge transformation in Hebridean living standards since the 1950s, but still highlighted the greater comfort – and warmth – of American houses. More important than practical issues, however, have been the spiritual and social benefits of community and family, including her first great-grandchild, born in October 2009.

> *I've had a most wonderful life here. God's providence in my experience has been marvellous for me. I have never regretted going to the US.*

Notes

1. The award of an entry visa to the United States was dependent on the applicant having first secured a sponsor who would stand surety for them until they had secured employment and could fend for themselves. Emigrants were allowed to take

only £5 out of the country to cover their expenses while in transit and on arrival.

2. Jim Wilkie, *Metagama: a journey from Lewis to the New World* (Edinburgh, 2001, first published 1987); Marjory Harper, 'Crofter colonists in Canada: an experiment in empire settlement in the 1920s', *Northern Scotland*, Vol. 14 (1994), pp. 69–108.
3. The 'war brides' may have been women who, having gone to the USA soon after the war, had made a trip back to Britain and were on their way back to their husbands and families. The so-called 'thousand dollar cure' was a common remedy for homesickness in the 1950s. See Barry Broadfoot, *The Immigrant Years: from Britain and Europe to Canada 1945–1967* (Vancouver, 1986).
4. Roy D. Chapin jun. (1915–2001) became Chairman and Chief Executive of American Motors Corporation, which he joined in 1954 when the corporation was formed. His father, Roy Chapin, as well as founding the Hudson Motor Car Company in 1908, was for nine months (August 1932 – March 1933) Secretary of Commerce in Herbert Hoover's administration.
5. The children did learn to read Gaelic when they attended school in Back for three months during sojourns in Lewis.
6. Free Church of Scotland, *Monthly Record*, September 1954, pp. 182–183.
7. There are four congregations in Canada – one in Toronto and three in Prince Edward Island.

9

ʚ

Two Hundred Years of Emigration from Barra and Adjacent Islands Between the 1750s and 1950s

Calum Macneil

Emigration has played a major and at times pivotal role in the history of the Barra islands. The outflow of people affected every village of Barra and every populated satellite island – to the south, Berneray, Mingulay, Pabbay, Sandray and Vatersay; to the north-east Hellisay, Gighay, Flodday and Fuiay. All witnessed the haemorrhage of their population at times. Some of these islands were repopulated only to lose their inhabitants after a few years. Indeed, some of them appear to have been little more than temporary holding bays until a suitable opportunity arrived to emigrate overseas.

An overview of these 200 years will show that the cause or reason for emigration varied and sometimes there were a number of factors involved which had a bearing on these decisions. Students of history will find a rich and varied catalogue of events which fuelled the engine of emigration. Parallel to these events were the human elements of desire for a better life, a loathing of the conditions at home, deceit by agents, desperation; and during one period coercion, persecution and outright brutality.

If we are to set aside earlier deportations and banishments for alleged misdemeanours, the story starts with thirty-one Barra soldiers who were conscripted to fight in the war against the French in America in the 1750s. With them in America was Lieutenant Roderick MacNeil [mac Ruairidh, Ruairidh 'Dhuibh'], heir apparent to Barra. These soldiers took part in the second siege of Louisburg, Cape Breton Island, which ended on 26 July 1758, after seven terrible weeks. After the siege, a Barra soldier, Donald òg MacNeil from Sandray, was on board a naval vessel in the Bras d'Or lake which gave chase to a French vessel. After a fruitless chase across the Atlantic, the British vessel proceeded to England to refit. Donald òg made his way back to Sandray. It is said that his vivid description in praise of the Bras d'Or was indelibly imprinted on the minds of his listeners, and was to play a major part in their desire to emigrate in later years.

After spending the winter with his wife and infant sons, Donald òg returned to America and is believed to have lost his life at Quebec in 1759, as did Lieutenant Roderick MacNeil. Indeed, according to Dr Walker only six of the soldiers had made it back alive to Barra by 1764, the rest having perished in America (a terrible attrition rate indeed). Of the six that made it back, some were to return to America to fight in the American War of Independence, and having survived that, returned again as emigrants to Nova Scotia.

By the time of Walker's visit in 1764, kelp production was starting to play a more important role in the lives of the people of Barra. Whatever its merits, it was dirty, laborious and an unhealthy life for little remuneration for the tenants of the landlord. This explains the attractions of the army and navy during this period. If you survived the fighting and disease abroad, you may have money and a pension – a distinct advantage if you wanted to emigrate. The other means of subsistence – raising black cattle and long line fishing for cod and ling – were uncertain and in the case of line fishing, salt was both difficult and expensive to get and the end product, the cured fish, had to be transported in open skiffs to Greenock and Port Glasgow. This was a daunting voyage around the Mull of Kintyre, although the opening of the Crinan Canal improved matters latterly.

In March 1772, about eight Barra families emigrated with the John MacDonald of Glen Aladale expedition on the *Alexander* to the island of St. John. The main reason for the South Uist tenants leaving was the religious persecution they had to suffer under the laird of Boisdale. It is probable that the very generous terms offered by Glen Aladale for land in the island of St. John would be a major attraction to any Barra family seeking a better life.

By 1775 more Barra soldiers had joined the few veterans of Louisburg and Quebec to fight for the British crown during the American War of Independence. Fighting with them this time was another Roderick MacNeil, son of Lieutenant Roderick MacNeil, who was laird of Barra, and later colonel. Although wounded, he survived this war. He owed his life to Calum MacNeil of Gighay, who faithfully tended his wounds. Calum MacNeil (mac Iain Ruairidh 'phiobair') was page with Lieutenant MacNeil at Quebec. At the end of hostility in 1783, it is clear that not all the surviving Barra soldiers came back. Some of the single soldiers took up offers from the crown of grants of land in Nova Scotia. This arrangement also suited the crown, as it left experienced soldiers living in Nova Scotia, where they could be called upon in any emergency.

Between 1790 and 1793, Barra emigrants arrived at Pictou along with those from South Uist and Arisaig, some going to St. John's Island, others settling around Pictou before moving towards Antigonish. Some persistent tales from this period indicate that some friction existed between the tenants and the laird, who had been brought up as a Protestant. It would appear that an increase in the Barra population necessitated the building of a larger chapel in a more convenient spot. When some of the tenants were surveying the land in preparation for building, they were challenged by the laird as to their purpose. When told of their plan, he turned them down flat, challenging the most able of them to fight (he had obviously recovered from his war wounds). The leader of the delegation contemptuously dismissed his offer, and told Colonel MacNeil that they would emigrate rather than put up with such behaviour. This is exactly what they did. Given that a significant number left at this period, the laird did all in his power, along with others of the landlord class, to discourage emigration. That this class of people had influence in the corridors of power is evident from the Passenger Act of 1803, which limited the number of passengers carried to one passenger for every two tons burden of the vessel. There was also a stipulation as to the minimum rations to be supplied for each voyage. Although the high proportion of deaths on some vessels between 1801 and 1802 galvanised the Highland Society of Edinburgh to put their weight behind the introduction of this act for humanitarian reasons, the beneficial effect of it for the landlords of the Western Islands and Highlands was the steep rise in fares. This put emigration beyond the means of the labouring class.

The kelp, which had become the main income of the laird of Barra, required a steady labour force. The more kelp produced, the more the laird's profits grew. Colonel MacNeil was now married to Jean Cameron of Fassiefearn and raising a family. He had a mansion built at Eoligarry to go with his perceived status as a landlord of means. The returns from the kelp produced in the summer months by his tenants, as a condition of their tenancy, were increasing his coffers on the back of cheap labour.

The colonel was on very bad terms with James Allan MacDonell, Roman Catholic priest of Barra from 1784. He was also on less than amicable terms with his second cousin James MacNeil, son of Eachan òg, tacksman of Earsary, and Roderick òg MacNeil son of tacksman of Brevig. His cousins were involved with Hugh Dunoon, emigration agent, in chartering ships to convey emigrants from Barra between 1801 and 1803. Several stories have been told about the laird's behaviour when the emigrants were being transported from Port na Mara in Castlebay. One account states that the colonel struck Ruairidh òg and when urged by his father to retaliate he declined, saying instead that he would strike anyone who raised a hand to his chief.

However, I heard a more likely account from an elderly lady in my own village who stated that the laird arrived from Eoligarry in a state of extreme rage. He had no sooner dismounted from his horse when he accosted James MacNeil whom he classed as the ring leader. He struck a full blooded blow without warning. James MacNeil retaliated instantly, leaving the laird in a heap (no respect or deference here). As my informant could trace her maternal ancestry back to the very area concerned, I'm inclined to believe her story, which had been handed down directly through the family. James MacNeil, his brother Hector Ban, his sisters and cousins from Brevig and hundreds of others left Barra during this time for Sydney and

Pictou. They dispersed from Pictou to the island of St. John, along the coast to Antigonish, then up the Bras d'Or and the coast of Cape Breton. From Sydney they also moved into the Bras d'Or from the opposite direction. The prologue to this period was that James MacNeil returned to Barra to organise more emigrants for the following season. Whilst on a voyage to Arisaig along with the Rev. James Allan MacDonell, the vessel piled up on this shore with the loss of all hands. According to oral tradition, it was said that the colonel shed no tears at the loss of two people who had stubbornly refused to bow to him, and had shown that there was an alternative – emigration.

It is also worth noting that some families from Barra had been recruited from 1780 through to the 1790s to work in David Dale's cotton mills at New Lanark. Despite the fact that Dale was a good employer for his time, not all families recruited stayed with him. Indeed, some of those who returned to Barra were among the emigrants of 1802, leaving Barra for the second time, with little prospect of returning should matters not be to their liking.

In the aftermath of the major exodus of 1801 to 1803, the laird was left in a state of rage, with his workforce much depleted. He was to entice new tenants from South Uist and further afield in order that the kelping shores were fully exploited for his benefit. An in-depth analysis of the 1810 to 1811 rental roll for the Estate of Barra exposes the cynicism of the colonel's land policy. The rents charged bore no relationship at all to the agricultural value of the land concerned, with the rent averaging between £5 and £6. The average family, who were expected to produce three tons of dry kelp each season at the rate of £2 per ton, would have to work flat out for three months to clear their rent. Fishing and agriculture suffered during these critical summer months.

The rental per tenant at Nask was £6:18:8 for very inferior land. In the 1980s, the writer was paying £7 rental in this same village. The rental for Hilsay was £75:10:0. Comparisons with the baptismal records for this period show that this rental covered the three islands of Hellisay, Gighay and Flodday. Calum MacNeil, the faithful servant who had served with the colonel and his father in the American wars, having raised an able family of eleven in Gighay, was paying £24 annual rent. He went on, in 1817, to emigrate as did two of his brothers from Rulios and Earsary. Two other brothers had left earlier in 1802 and they all settled in Cape Breton. Roderick Ban MacNeil, another son of Hector òg tacksman of Earsary, was paying £18 for half of Hellisay, the other half being rented to Donald MacKinnon. Four of Roderick Ban's eight sons were also to leave Barra, three going to Cape Breton and one to Australia. Donald MacKinnon's sons also emigrated to Cape Breton after trying to eke out an existence around the shores of Northbay and Bruernish point.

Of the tenants of Flodday, between 1810 and 1811, John MacKinnon went to Cape Breton, and Archie MacMillan's children went to Cape Breton. It is not certain if Archie or his wife emigrated. These three islands totalled 687 acres of rock and bog with little ground for tilling, yet the total rental was £75:10 shillings. It is true that line fishing and harpooning of basking shark were conducted successfully from the excellent Acarsaid between Hellisay and Gighay. But when we compare the rental for Vatersay, which totalled £74:2:6 for 2,338 acres, one is left completely baffled. Four tenants at Caolis were paying £14:2:6 between them. Donald MacNeil, the tacksman (the colonel's brother in law), was paying £60 for Vatersay farm. Vatersay is much larger than the northern islands of the Barra group and is vastly superior in agricultural terms. It is true that the colonel and his brother in law were of the same religion, but it is more likely that family ties explain the easy terms when compared to others. One would have thought more of the laird had he shown the same generosity towards the man who saved his life in America, by daily cleaning his wounds.

The period between 1803 and 1817 saw a big reduction in emigration from Barra, although evidence from land records in Nova Scotia, Cape Breton and St. John's Island, along with census material and oral tradition, shows that there was a steady trickle managing to go mostly via Tobermory.

The end of the Napoleonic War started the decline of kelp prices, leading to a virtual collapse by the 1820s, from a peak of £22 per ton to the landlord, to a price which could not even cover the derisory cost of the labour. Soldiers and sailors returning to Barra, this time from the Napoleonic wars and the navy, had some money but no prospects at home. The disgruntled kelp workers form the other ingredient in this volatile mix. Emigration agents, like Simon Fraser, would have little difficulty in signing up recruits. Given the circumstances, and despite some hiccups, mostly of Fraser's insincerity, up to 400 people departed from Greenock for Cape Breton on the *William Tell*, the *Hope* and the *Ann*. The conditions promised were neither met whilst on passage, nor were they honoured by Fraser when they arrived at Sydney. It was the intervention of the Lieutenant Governor of Cape Breton, George Ainslie, which saved the day. His letter to the Earl of Bathurst, Secretary of State for the Colonial Department, is reproduced in Fr. Allan MacMillan's very informative book *To the Hill of Boisdale*. Ainslie arranged for the new arrivals to be shipped, with all their baggage, up the Bras d'Or to the vicinity of Grand Narrows where their countrymen were well settled.

According to George Ainslie, they would be well received by people of unbounded hospitality (Barra emigrants who had already settled there). It was prior to this emigration that the laird expressed some regret, in a letter dated 6 June 1816 to Angus MacDonald, parish priest in Barra, whilst fishing for some information in Liverpool regarding emigration, that it was distressing to his feelings that people to whom he was much attached should leave him, but if it was for their own good he would regret it less. He may have been mellowing with age! But it is also likely that given the slide of the kelp prices, which would be irreversible, the demand for tenants and kelp labourers would be much less. The people of Barra, able or otherwise, were voting with their feet and it is quite apparent from the tone of his correspondence with the priest that emigrants did not think the colonel any more trustworthy than the emigration agents (what a richly deserved slap in the face).

Despite the difficulties which faced the emigrants of 1817 at Sydney, Cape Breton, letters being received back from Cape Breton must have been encouraging enough, because, leading up to the big emigration between 1821 and 1822, via Tobermory, those intending to emigrate were advancing small amounts of cash to a Captain Barge. Possibly to cover their fares to Tobermory, they were also selling their shares in fishing boats as the time of departure drew near. It is evident their decision to go was well planned in advance; matters were certainly not improving in Barra. Among the emigrants of this period were the MacKenzies of Kentangaval and Lower Glen, on whom the colonel commented favourably in one of his letters. Also among those emigrating was the extensive family of Iain òg MacKinnon, who although living initially at Gortein, had spread to Caolis, Nask, Kentangaval and Glen.

The evidence of the industriousness of the MacKinnons is still to be seen in their dykes, reaching up the lower slopes of Beinn a Sguid, Beinn Bhreac, Beinn Mhoir and Beinn a Lochainn with all available ground tilled. The old man, with his second wife and his nine married children, and the widow of one of his sons, all crossed the ocean to seek a better life.

Colonel MacNeil died in 1822. It was clear that despite his mansion in Eoligarry, he was spending a great deal of his time on the mainland and it appears that he did not even visit Barra every year. The colonel had his admirers, amongst them the minister of Barra, the Rev. Edmund MacQueen, from 1774 to 1813, the priest Rev. Angus MacDonald from 1805 to 1826, and some Barra folk reminiscing fondly in their dotage. Some scholars and historians of the last century '*cha tuig thu an duinne gu bith da gnothach ris*', and the Barra tenants who crossed the ocean may not have been so fulsome in their praise. It is the opinion of the writer that, although the colonel may have been a fine soldier, he most certainly was not a prudent businessman. He was living far beyond his means, and had no compunction in ratcheting up his tenants' rents to finance his lifestyle. He had, as a soldier, fought alongside some of his subsequent tenants, but did them no favours afterwards. Indeed there is evidence to that effect from oral traditions of the family of one Hector MacNeil (mac Sheumais ic Alisdair ic Ruairidh Dhuidh), another second cousin of the laird. Hector had gone to work in Glasgow in the 1790s but things did not work out for him. He had lost four young children in infancy. He met the colonel in Glasgow and was offered a croft and other inducements to return, which he did. One day, after spending a long hard day on the kelp shore, he returned to find that the colonel's servants had appropriated his poultry in order to feed some unexpected guests. After giving the laird a piece of his mind, Hector upped sticks again, emigrating in 1802 and settling in Cape Breton, where, happily, he and his wife and family prospered.

Had the colonel genuinely felt for his kinsfolk he could have lived more frugally and led by example. He was, after all, interested in land improvements, despite which there would still have been those who wanted to emigrate. They would, however, have had more money to go out with, and there would have been less disruption and bitterness. He could have written constructively on their behalf, instead of shedding crocodile tears latterly. Then there is the will with its quite delusionary terms. Any sensible person reading it would have to feel some sympathy for his son and heir (later General Roderick MacNeil) who was not only saddled with an estate in debt but also beneficiaries who appeared reluctant to take a reduction in their entitlements.

It appears to be at the very beginning of his incumbency that the township of Kial and Kilbar were cleared in order to create the home farm of Eoligarry. Those evicted were left hanging on like limpets around Ardveenish, Huileibhagh and Leachd nan Torr. Whatever his intentions it is clear from correspondence between him and Angus MacDonald, the priest in Barra, that the young laird was in a hurry to change things. Quite early on he was displaying a volatile nature and being something of a control freak. As early as 1824 he was threatening not only his tenants with expulsion but also their adult children. It would appear that the kelpers were in sullen rebellion probably because they were expected to do the same work for less remuneration. A lowering of market price meant a squeeze on the producer, in this case the labourer, whereas the middleman (the laird) did all in his power to maximise his share of the reduced value.

The fishermen were also the subject of his displeasure. Those in Sandray got a special mention. The theme was all about control of resources, and a curtailment of what little independence the population strove for. Between 1826 and 1827 more chose emigration to Cape Breton as the answer to their troubles. The laird was embarking on a major alkali works at Northbay with the aim of adding value to his kelp by refining prior to shipment. This was intended to enable the island product to compete on price with cheap foreign imports. To finance the venture, along with borrowed money, were some swingeing increases in rents. By 1833 some township rents had doubled and even trebled. Nask had risen from £20:16:0 in total to £70; and Kilbar, Kial and Vaslain had gone from £225:5:0 in total to £820 for what were now the farms of Eoligarry and Vaslain. The rental for Vatersay and Caolis had increased from £74:2:6 to £550, all this in a space of twenty-two years in a declining economy. To provide the labour for the new venture, all able-bodied men were removed from the southern islands to Barra (these islands do not appear on the 1833 rental). The laird also carried out his threat of May 1824, to replace disgruntled Catholic tenants with Protestants. The 1836 rent roll shows people from Tiree and North Uist now in place, with concentrations on the best arable land on the west side.

The alkali works were an expensive failure that soon led to the sequestration of the estate when the creditors pulled the plug. This, along with the bad harvests between 1835 and 1837, was the impetus for more emigrations, again to the maritime provinces of Canada – despite the facts that not only was each wave of emigrants now poorer, but in addition land was becoming scarcer in Cape Breton. When Colonel Gordon of Cluny became landlord, following a very short honeymoon period, matters started to deteriorate and to the best of my knowledge 1843 would have been the last sizable emigration to Cape Breton.

The potato blight was the next blow for the increasingly demoralised and impoverished population. By 1848 starvation was stalking each hamlet. Evicted tenants from the west side were now adding to the pressures on the marginal land of the east side. The townships of Rulios, Earsary and Skallary, which saw an increase in tenants from ten in 1811 to eighteen in 1836, were now swamped with the displaced. Brevig, where the number of tenants had increased from ten in 1811 to twenty-three in 1836, was now also under pressure from more cottars. Bruernish, which had nine tenants in 1811 and seventeen tenants by 1836, was in addition now under even more pressure. By 1841, some 108 people were living on Hellisay (although I suspect that Gighay was included). There were only three families in 1811. Most were families evicted from Kilbar and Kial between 1822 and 1824, along with cottars from Bogach and Bruernish. They were evicted again by 1850, this time to Eriskay. The story in townships like Glen was similar. It does not even feature in the 1810–11 roll, but by 1837 there were twenty-five tenants. By 1848, each and every township was trying to cope with greatly increased numbers. The landlord's solution to what was undeniably a crisis was brutal and without compassion. The policy now was one of expulsion.

By 1848, Barra folk were arriving on the mainland and continued to do so in great numbers until 1851. The methods used by Gordon's hirelings and those in whom authority was invested were truly despicable, with his underdogs vying with each other as to who could be the most petty and cruel to defenceless and destitute people. The condition of the refugees when they reached Tobermory, Glasgow, Edinburgh, the Inverness area and Nairn was one which shocked the authorities.

The year 1851 saw the transport of up to 450 people from Barra to Quebec via Lochboisdale. Their condition on arrival at the quarantine station on Ile de Grosse raised a good deal of anger in Canada. Despite the master of the *Admiral* and his wife doing their utmost for them on passage, they were scantily clothed and malnourished and therefore not fit to cope with a Canadian winter. Those who tried to escape prior to embarkation in Barra were hunted down with hounds. Some, who managed to evade capture, ended up traumatised, split forever from their families. In my own young days, elderly people could still relate a vivid picture told by their elders of the horrors inflicted on old and young by ground constables and others, in their concerted drive to rid the estate of the 'problem', as they saw it.

The Tiree folk who had arrived in Barra in the 1830s were subjected to the worst of the treatment, most of them being evicted during this period. It was during these evictions that the Church of Scotland minister, Henry Beatson, was to be exposed as a wolf in sheep's clothing, in sharp contrast to his predecessors. Henry Beatson had donned the mantle of the landlord's arch disciple. He was seen actively orchestrating the hired thugs as they went about their dirty business of expulsions. This indeed was Barra's darkest hour.

The potato blight had also struck Cape Breton during the same period. This meant that Barra emigrants were destined to go on to Ontario. It is ominous that the writer and others have had little success in finding a concentration of Barra folk from this period. Although the spectre of mass emigration was not to be seen on Barra again until the early 1920s, Barra folk would still go to seek a better life on the mainland, but mostly as individual families. Some would come back, as did a few of those who went to the mainland between 1848 and 1850. The herring fishing, which took off in a big way from the end of the 1860s, was to play a major role in lifting the population off their knees. From a downtrodden, demoralised group they were to rise up in increasing militancy to fight for justice. They were to witness and participate in the Napier Commission hearings. They were to gain security of tenure and went on to raid the farms to regain some measure of redress for the treatment meted out to their forbears.

The men folk by the 1850s had turned increasingly to the merchant service and some followed this employment even during the boom years of the herring fishing. The women, who had started to work as agricultural labourers on the mainland from the 1850s, had now become expert gutters, following the herring shoals around the British Isles. Others worked in service in the towns. The First World War took a high toll on the men folk. The herring boats, which were still only sailing fifies, scaffies and zulus, had been laid up on the shore. By the end of hostilities they had deteriorated to a great degree. There was no capital available either to repair or replace them. The Bolshevik Revolution had put paid to the Baltic markets. The heroes had returned but not to a land of plenty. Andrew MacDonell, a Roman Catholic priest with connections to Canada and the C.P.R., started to recruit potential emigrants, ostensibly to address the population scarcity on the Canadian prairie.

The emigrations of 1922 to 1924 to Alberta attracted a substantial amount of recruit families; and it is clear from the age of some of the heads of families that they were hoping for a brighter future not for themselves, but for their children. As the off-lying islands to the south and north-east had all been abandoned before the war, only the main islands of Barra and Vatersay were affected. There were pockets of people from most of the townships now settling in Red Deer and ClanDonald. The conditions on the prairie were certainly not what had been promised and some became disillusioned whilst struggling with life there. By the mid to late 1930s some had started to drift to the west coast, mostly around the Vancouver area, where steady work for a wage could be had. A lot felt very embittered towards Andrew MacDonell. This bitterness for MacDonell was also felt by their relations and acquaintances in Barra. Some, of course, did succeed on the prairie. I have read a report from Canada which tends to excuse Andrew MacDonell, placing the blame on agents on this side of the Atlantic, and on the emigration scheme, for attracting too many, resulting in inadequate preparation on the Canadian side for their reception. My own conversation with some of the emigrant families in the Vancouver area in the 1960s, including my father's first cousins, would leave one in no doubt that they felt misled and blamed MacDonell for the deception. There were no more emigrations of this type from Barra again, although in the 1950s two families from 'Sgor nan Druidean', with children still at school, left for Australia, amongst them my wife's aunt and her husband who was a first cousin of my mother.

Thus the 200 years of emigration were to end. The foregoing goes a long way to explaining why, along with the sailors who jumped ship, so many people all over the world regard the tiny island of Barra as their spiritual home. The reasons for emigrating, especially in the early years, were undoubtedly to seek a better life and by and large that is what happened. In Cape Breton they got large grants of land and were free from the yoke of landlords. They were not afraid of hard work, and despite the fact that by 1817 they had a new church at Craigston, they chose to emigrate to a land where churches and clergy were exceedingly thin on the ground. They were to experience out-migration to the Boston area by the 1860s, as the farms could not retain everyone. From Boston, some were to move to the west coast of America. The mining towns of Cape Breton were to attract more folk off the land, as the money economy became more important.

The close-knit Gaelic-speaking communities were being eroded and dispersed. This would be keenly felt by the older folk, who although not treated well in Barra, took their language and culture with them and were immensely proud of their heritage. In Cape Breton especially, they shared the heritage and culture of a Gaelic-speaking people. They were surrounded by islanders and highlanders. It is a fact that they would not have achieved as much had they stayed in an island that would be increasingly overcrowded, with little opportunity. They and their families would only have been held back. They were diligent, stoic, resourceful and deserved to succeed. Few, if any, came back from these early emigrations. The same was not true of the 1922 to 1924 emigrants, some of whom became disenchanted with life on the prairie. Amongst those who returned was a man, with his family, who had been an avid supporter of the scheme. He had urged people to sign up, but had a terrible reality check. One of my grandfather's brother's five sons also came back. His parents died in Canada as eventually did his siblings. This had also been an emigration of hope.

There are instances from the earlier emigrations of one member of the family being left behind, perhaps in some cases to look after ageing grandparents. In the case of the family of Ewen MacSween from Upper Borve, the eldest son, who was married and moved from Caolis to Sandray, stayed in Barra. In the case of my own great-great-great-grandfather, Alexander MacLean, from Druideal, the youngest son stayed in Barra, although he was single when the rest left. There were also instances of the occasional person changing their mind at the last minute. There is the story of one family from the 1923 emigration, the head of whom was not the type to hurry, with 'laid back' being a family trait. When the steamer arrived to transport the emigrants to Lochboisdale, a neighbour hurried to inform this worthy to make haste. He found the intending emigrant relaxing on the 'beinge' smoking his pipe, and despite the fact that most of the furniture had been sold in preparation, he told the concerned neighbour that he had let the idea of going abroad out of his head.

The story of emigration by its very nature cannot be simple, nor can it be a story of mere statistics, for it is a human story. Some of the emigrants lost the heads of their families on the voyage. A lot had to bear the heartache of burial at sea for children who died on passage, with some of their hopes buried with them. The 'cianalas' would affect those leaving in many ways, and those left behind would miss forever more those who emigrated. Young romances would be terminated, sometimes for ever. In Cape Breton news of home would be eagerly awaited, as new waves of emigrants arrived.

For those seeking to reach a definitive figure for emigration over these 200 years, the task can be very difficult. Whereas, for some years, figures can be accepted as fairly accurate, I have great difficulty accepting some totals for between 1801 and 1803. For example, cross reference can cast doubt, as I have found in genealogy books. Families from Barra have been given an emigration date of 1802, whereas in reality they did not leave Barra until the 1820s. There are similar erroneous claims for other emigrations. Given that we have a reasonably accurate population for 1764 it would be stretching credulity a bit for the natural increase to sustain the levels claimed. However, we do know that immigrants into Barra from elsewhere, to replace departures, would then join in subsequent emigrations to the new world from Barra. Therefore, it would be unwise to try and fit the numbers into tidy boxes. Even the lowest estimates show that emigration played a major role in Barra's history.

In conclusion, the southern half of Barra, which was the part still in the ownership of Lady Gordon Cathcart, was, after protracted negotiations, bought by Robert Lister MacNeil. He was an American descendant of Hector Ban MacNeil who had emigrated in 1803. Aside from his duties as landlord, Robert Lister MacNeil wasted no time in pursuing his passion for the restoration of Kisimul Castle. By the late 1960s this task was completed. He was laid to rest in his beloved castle. The restored ruins had now become a beacon not only for returning MacNeils but for others as well. Iain Roderick MacNeil succeeded his father. He recently offered the estate to the community, and until this offer is taken up, the caretakers are the present equivalent of the Scottish Department of Agriculture and Fisheries. The onerous task of keeping 'a castle in the sea' in repair has now been entrusted to Historic Scotland, on long-term lease. One has to conclude that the tenures of Iain Roderick MacNeil, and his father Robert Lister, were much happier times for the tenants of Barra – not just because we live in different times, but because of their own demeanour.

10

ᴕ

Some Final Thoughts: Enigmas in Hebridean Emigration

Marjory Harper

Numerous visual images speak poignantly of the clearance, exile and homesickness of highland emigrants. Among the best known are Thomas Faed's painting *The Last of the Clan* (1865) and that by John Watson Nicol, *Lochaber No More* (1883), both of which reflect the sadness of parting from kin and country, while *A Coronach in the Backwoods* (1859), by George W. Simson, depicts the anguish of a pioneer settler and his wife on receiving news from the homeland.[1] From a later era, photographs of the departure of the *Metagama* from Stornoway in 1923 demonstrate the huge contemporary fascination with an emigrant ship which, to this day, remains synonymous with the twentieth-century haemorrhage from the Outer Hebrides.[2] So powerful – and firmly-rooted in highland soil – are images of clearance and exile, that they have dominated perceptions of Scottish emigration as a whole since the late eighteenth century, even though from the 1860s an ever-increasing majority of participants came from the urban-industrial lowlands.

This paper explores some of the paradoxes and enigmas inherent in two centuries of Hebridean emigration. It scrutinizes the interaction of exile and entrepreneurship, necessity and choice, failure and success, with reference to four particular periods: the first phase of clearance-related emigration in the late eighteenth and early nineteenth centuries; the 'high noon' of eviction and exile and its aftermath as the region was battered, initially by post-war depression and then by potato famine from the 1820s to the 1850s; the decade of economic dislocation that generated unprecedented depopulation in the aftermath of the First World War; and the post-1945 era, when emigration occurred in a context of increasing globalization. Centre-stage is given to the neglected twentieth-century story.

Socio-economic Transformation: The First Phase of Clearance

One of the enigmas of the late eighteenth century, when landlords and government were intent on modernizing the highlands, was the extent to which emigrants departed willingly. It is well known that observers such as Samuel Johnson and James Boswell deplored the depopulation, as did numerous contributors to *The Statistical Account of Scotland*. While Johnson admitted that individuals might well improve their circumstances by going to America, he deplored the effect on the nation of the highlanders' 'epidemick disease of wandering'.[3] Two decades later, the minister of North Uist complained that 'flattering accounts' sent back by islanders who had emigrated made others 'resolve to desert their native country, and to encounter the dangers of crossing the Atlantic to settle in the wilds of America'.[4] Emigration agents such as

Thomas Douglas, Fifth Earl of Selkirk, were vilified, and the Passenger Vessels Act of 1803 was a disingenuous attempt to undermine their recruiting activities, although Selkirk managed to slip under the radar and dispatch three shiploads of 800 highlanders to Prince Edward Island just before the legislation was implemented.[5]

The grey area concerns the attitude of the emigrants. Did they see their decisions in a positive or negative light? St Andrew's Channel, the strip of water separating the communities of Iona and Christmas Island in the middle of the Bras d'Or, Cape Breton's large inland lake, is commonly known as the Barra Strait. The land on either side of the narrows was settled by the families and descendants of soldiers from Barra, who had been impressed by its potential as they sailed up the lake after the siege of Louisburg in 1758. Of course, these tacksmen-officers would not have been in the British army in the first place if their traditional way of life had not been disrupted by the same sort of upheavals that subsequently persuaded the fellow islanders whom they recruited that their traditions – and their extended communities – were more likely to be preserved across the Atlantic than in the Hebrides. And while reports from Skye in the 1770s seem to indicate something of a mania for emigration, it was a mania that had been generated in large part by the domestic dislocation caused by landlord instigated modernization policies. The dance called America, witnessed by Johnson and Boswell when they visited Armadale in 1773, symbolized a mixture of positive community-based enterprise and the erosion of a traditional way of life.[6]

The High Noon of Exile: Famine, Eviction and Expatriation

The initial phase of clearance-related emigration has sometimes been airbrushed out of the narrative of the highland diaspora, eclipsed by – or conflated with – the succeeding era, when landlords promoted rather than obstructed emigration and the Hebridean haemorrhage was much more emphatically associated with exile. The end of the Napoleonic wars triggered both the collapse of the fragile highland economy, especially the kelp industry, and the bankruptcy of many estates. In 1838 Colonel John Gordon of Cluny in Aberdeenshire purchased the islands of Barra and South Uist and a decade later became perhaps the most notorious evictor of his age, sending 3,200 tenants to Canada between 1849 and 1851. His activities were graphically documented by contemporary commentators and eyewitnesses, who described the mayhem during the so-called 'transporting season', as unwilling emigrants were pursued across the machair by constables, handcuffed and dragged aboard vessels anchored in Loch Boisdale.[7] Also legendary in the annals of mid-nineteenth-century eviction and emigration is the story of the clearance of Boreraig and Suishnish in Skye in 1853. It is remembered because the 'strange wailing sound' of the evicted crofters was heard – and documented – by the geologist Sir Archibald Geikie, and because seventy-five of those evicted were sent to Australia aboard the ill-fated ship *Hercules*, on which sixty-five passengers died of typhus and smallpox.[8]

Yet even in that unambiguously traumatic era of potato famine and forced emigration, there are paradoxes. The Upper Canadian commentator Adam Hope was sceptical about the extent of the emigrants' poverty. 'The highlanders', he wrote in a letter to his brother in 1849, 'are not *ashamed* to let you know that they are *paupers* and to make themselves out poorer than they are. In changing some one pound Scotch Bank Notes in our stores they let us understand they durst not allow their notes to be seen in Scotland or they would not have got their passage paid!! In less than five years you will find that their Highland pride won't allow them to acknowledge that they got their passage paid.'[9]

The dominant and persistent image, however, was one of the emigrants as victims. It was an image reinforced by many of the witnesses to the Napier Commission in 1883, and by reports of the experiences of the seventy-eight families from Lewis, Harris and North Uist who – with limited government funding – were relocated at Killarney and Saltcoats on the Canadian prairies in 1888 and 1889.[10] During an official visit to the infant Killarney colony in 1890, the Countess of Aberdeen declared, 'May Heaven preserve us from ever being fated to banishment to the far-famed wheatlands of Manitoba. Oh the inexpressible dreariness of these everlasting prairies... The struggle to live has swallowed up all the energy.'[11] Some time later T. J. Lawlor, the Killarney merchant who dealt with the settlers, claimed that their limited success was due to their monolingualism and self-imposed isolation. 'Gaelic may be a very nice and expressive dialect (sic) but you cannot raise wheat from it, and these people had nothing else', was his observation.[12] On the other hand, the Napier Commission's published evidence included a collection of rather formulaic promotional letters written by a handful of crofters from Benbecula who in 1883 had been sent by Lady Emily Gordon Cathcart (daughter-in-law of the notorious Colonel Gordon) to establish a settlement near Wapella, then in the North-West Territories.[13]

The Inter-war Era: The *Metagama* and the *Marloch*

Scotland's haemorrhage of population showed no signs of abating with the turn of the century. The years just before the First World War saw an upsurge in departures, particularly to Canada, then in the decade following the 1921 census the country's actual population fell by 0.8 per cent, the decline being most marked in the highland counties: 13.8 per cent.[14] The 1920s remains the only period since records began when Scotland's actual population has declined absolutely between censuses, as the numbers leaving (by no means all for overseas destinations) outstripped the natural increase. Most of the emigrants came from the central belt, but the well-documented departure of two Canadian Pacific liners from the Outer Hebrides within a single week in April 1923 made a huge and lasting impact on public awareness well beyond the affected islands. On Sunday 15 April, the *Marloch* left Lochboisdale with 280 emigrants from Benbecula, South Uist, Barra and Vatersay, bound for Alberta, and six days later the *Metagama* embarked 315 Hebrideans, all but fifteen from Lewis, for Ontario.[15]

Many enigmas are embedded in the story of Hebridean and highland emigration in the 1920s, not least the decision by the Canadian government to open a third Scottish emigration office in 1923. Along with the older agencies in Glasgow and Aberdeen, it catered for the considerable interest in Canada in inter-war Scotland, but in a highland context it could be seen as a paradoxical trend, given the long-standing antagonism of highlanders – and particularly Hebrideans – to emigration, for the clearances of the first half of the nineteenth century and the crofters' war of the 1880s had certainly not been forgotten by later generations.

In many respects, the state of the highlands and islands in 1918 resembled that at the end of the Napoleonic wars a century earlier. The area was beset by economic crisis, with farming and fishing in turmoil, the spectre of famine, special government investigations, financial assistance to emigrants, and active recruitment agents. The new ingredient was the islanders' apparently more positive attitude to emigration as a remedy for their plight, a surprising reaction which was arguably attributable to the interplay of three sets of circumstances: changing expectations, acceptable opportunities, and the services of professional facilitators.

To some extent, of course, the emigrants' expectations were negative, in the sense that relocation overseas could be seen as a last, desperate resort or protest against the prospect of starvation, fear at alarmingly high rates of tuberculosis, and frustration at the tardiness of land settlement schemes. Moreover, the tragic loss of the troop ship *Iolaire* off Stornoway in the early hours of 1 January 1919 had cast a deep gloom over the Isle of Lewis in particular, and helped to push some people in the direction of making a fresh start, away from haunting memories.[16] At the same time, however, the war had broadened the horizons of islanders, particularly ex-servicemen. During their travels they had been able to compare the subsistence lifestyle of the Hebrides with more comfortable conditions elsewhere and had begun to realize that some of their problems were simply the result of the insurmountable physical limitations of their environment. And as crofting legislation and state pensions began to offer a measure of security to elderly parents, it became easier for the younger generation to leave and seek their fortunes elsewhere. That they were ambivalent about the decision to emigrate is demonstrated in a quayside photograph of a family group of emigrants, whose apprehensive expressions belie the optimistic sentiments of the placard they are displaying, with its declaration that they are about to embark on 'the crofter's trail to happiness'.

Anticipation of a better life overseas was integrally related to the acceptable opportunities that opened up in the 1920s in the shape of assisted emigration to the dominions offered under the Empire Settlement Act of 1922. Unlike previous legislation, the Act applied to the whole of the UK, and did not single out the highlanders as particular recipients of charity. Recruitment took place under collective nomination, whereby emigrants were given advances of up to 75 per cent of the £16 ocean fare, and the decision to have some of the liners call at the islands in 1923 and 1924 was made in a deliberate attempt to save impoverished Hebrideans the extra expense of travelling to Glasgow to embark.[17]

The third ingredient in the emergence of more positive attitudes was the high profile role of recruitment agents, who initially persuaded the emigrants to leave, and then organized their departure. Such agency activity was not new, of course: with their illustrated lectures, colourful posters and persuasive pamphlets, competing agents had been a familiar sight in the Hebrides since at least the 1870s. In Lewis, the key individual was William Noxon, agent-general for Ontario, who organized the *Metagama*'s Hebridean passengers. His counterpart in the southern Hebrides was Father Andrew MacDonell, a character who undoubtedly constitutes one of the central enigmas in the story of inter-war emigration from Scotland.

A product of the Abbey School at Fort Augustus, MacDonell had worked as a mission priest in the area around Glenurquhart and Glenmoriston until 1912, when, in an abrupt, unexplained change of career, he retooled as an emigration agent, organizing the removal of British orphans to Ladysmith in Vancouver Island. After war service in France, during which he won the Military Cross, he returned to Canada and got himself onto the payroll of the Canadian immigration department in order to recruit Hebridean Catholics for a planned colony in northern Alberta. In selecting and marshalling recruits, he enlisted the help of priests in the islands, including Donald McIntyre, the priest in Castlebay, but the whole venture, which by the end of the decade had seen him transfer approximately 1,350 emigrants to Canada, was fraught with controversy. Although in 1955, towards the end of his long life, MacDonell received the MBE for his 'services to emigration', he generated discontent and ire on all sides: among his recruits, who claimed they had been swindled; within the Catholic hierarchy in Scotland, which felt tainted by association with his schemes; with the Canadian immigration authorities, who were constantly frustrated at his carelessness and over-commitment; and in the British Labour Party, which believed that assisted emigration was a political ploy to stave off the introduction of state welfare. To this day, the perception of MacDonell as a traitor lingers in South Uist and Barra, primarily because – wittingly or not – he was doing the bidding of the aggressively anti-Catholic proprietor of those islands, Lady Emily Gordon Cathcart. Emigration had for long been the estate management's favourite weapon against unwanted tenants, and Lady Cathcart's enthusiasm for colonizing the prairies was shaped not by a concern for the colonists' welfare but possibly by her share-holding interests in the Canadian Pacific Railway and the Hudson's Bay Company, as well as her determination to remove Catholic crofters.[18]

Morag Bennett, nee Macleod (1913–2008) was one of those who sailed on the *Marloch*. Aged ten when she left Benbecula with her parents and six siblings, she was in her mid-nineties when interviewed at her home in Sechelt, British Columbia. She was emphatic that her parents' decision had been triggered by the fact that 'there was nothing there in Benbecula for the family', which, unusually for those on the *Marloch*, was a Protestant family. In conversation, she reflected on the voyage, adjustments and hardships:

> *Oh, I remember the blasting of the fog horn for sure, I can still hear it. And of course we didn't – we were put in the state rooms, you know, to sleep, and that – and we never had running water in Benbecula, as you know, it was just a well, and we didn't know what the bowl and the taps and all this sort of things were, you know....*
>
> *Oh well, you know, I was young, and I thought it was great, especially the winter, I loved the snow, you know, big drifts and playing in the snow, but you must remember, I was just ten years old, but my parents, my mother brought a few plants from Benbecula, and of course she didn't know that the winter was so cold, and they all froze, the first frost in the winter....*
>
> *The houses were very small, cause they all had big families, that was the idea, to bring out the big families, and get the prairies settled. And the houses were just sort of like a square box, and not insulated at all. So you can imagine. Terrible. We had to cut the wood. My father had to – and he was in his 70s, for gosh sakes. He had to cut the trees and poplar trees for wood, to keep us warm. Boy, I tell you, it was a terrible time....*

> *The Hebrideans didn't know how to farm properly. You know what I mean? The Russian ones, that had the good farms, they knew what they were doing, but from what I can think back on now, the Hebrideans didn't know.*[19]

During the Depression of the 1930s Morag's family moved west to British Columbia, where she met her husband and stayed for the rest of her life.

Meanwhile, on the other side of the world, in New South Wales, Angus MacDonald, a native of Lochmaddy, was interviewed in 1987 as part of the New South Wales Bicentennial Oral History Project. Born in 1905, he emigrated in 1926 for adventure, after a recruitment agent from Australia House had visited Lochmaddy. Angus had already heard about Australia from his late father, who had been to the Antipodes as a merchant mariner and who dropped dead on board ship in Hong Kong harbour in the year that Angus emigrated. After undertaking a six-month preparatory course at Clayden training school in Ipswich, Angus sailed for Sydney, where he worked as a gardener until he was laid off during the Depression and subsequently found himself living in a hostel for destitute men for three to four years. In 1947, following war service, he married a widow whom he had met through the Scottish Society, but he later divorced her because she was – like his own father – an alcoholic. When asked how he met his wife, Angus recounted:

> *Oh, through the Scottish society … I joined the Highland Society when I first came to Australia, I joined the Highland Society… We used to hold our gathering at the Showground every year, which was a big – big – big affair in them days. And at that time they had a Scottish concert. See they had the Highland concert up at the Town Hall on New Year's night.*[20]

Emigrant Voices: Hebridean Emigration After the Second World War

The experiences of the Murray family from Shader in Lewis – Calum and Cathie in particular – straddle the two eras of inter-war and post-war emigration. Before the First World War their father had worked on grain elevators at Thunder Bay (formerly Fort William), Ontario. After returning to Lewis to marry in 1917, he went back to Canada in 1924, and three years later he was joined by his wife and five children, who sailed on the *Melita*. By then he had moved to Prince Rupert, British Columbia, where he was killed in an accident in 1932. His widow brought the children back to Lewis, where they recalled being ridiculed at school for their Canadian accents, but the wanderlust gene had been passed on to the younger generation. After service in the merchant navy, Calum followed in his father's footsteps, and for thirty years, from 1953 to 1983, he was a transatlantic commuter, spending his summers freighting grain on the Great Lakes and his winters back in Lewis with his wife Jessie and their children. Cathie, meanwhile, looked further afield. While she and her sister Chrissie were working with the NAAFI in Germany after the war, she had a chance encounter with a young woman from New Zealand, who persuaded her to go out under the £10 passage scheme in 1948:

> *So anyway, while I was over in Germany I met a New Zealand girl. But meanwhile, I thought, I was aiming for Canada all the time, and I wrote Canada House, got no answer, so this Betty, she says to me, 'You go to New Zealand, you see what they're doing there'. So, to cut a long story short, they, they answered right off, and all I had to do was fill the forms and you could go over there for TEN POUNDS.*

And – of course – you had to work with them for two years, which was the best ten years – ten pounds – I ever spent.[21]

After two years in Wellington, Cathie moved north to Auckland, where she would have stayed, if she had not come home after sixteen years to look after her elderly mother. She returned to Lewis by a circuitous route:

Oh, I wanted a job where I'd be free to roam, and I worked in the, first of all I worked in the hostel I lived in, in the cafeteria there. That's while I was in Wellington, I did my two years there that was where they sent me. And then I went up, I'd met up with Australian girls, and they had gone up to Auckland. 'Oh, why don't you come up here?' They'd started working in hospitals, and here I get another job up there, in a cafeteria in the nurses' home. Well, I was there for nearly twelve years, and that's when I started the rolling stone. I went back, working my way back, got a permit and worked in the States for two years, Canada two years, back home.[22]

For the Murrays, emigration was very much an adventure as well as a practicality. But while both Cathie and Calum ultimately returned to Lewis, many others did not. Murdo Macivor lives in Vancouver. He was born in Arnol, Lewis, in January 1932. After leaving school at the age of fifteen, he worked as a weaver for two years until, like so many of his fellow islanders, he joined the merchant navy. He subsequently spent a year with the Anchor Line, transporting Scottish emigrants from Glasgow to Australia, and another year on vessels taking emigrants from Liverpool to New Zealand. In 1953 a back injury that he had sustained while working for MacBrayne's flared up while he was on a voyage up the Pacific coast, and he found himself under the surgeon's knife in Vancouver. By the time he had recovered his ship was long gone, but he had already fallen in love with Vancouver and took steps to stay there:

> *Anyway the day I went up to see the emigration man, 'Oh,' he said, 'oh you've been here since the 1st of August', he says. 'What were you up to?' 'Oh,' I says, 'I was in the hospital and I just got clearance on Friday', so this was Monday, I believe. 'Oh' and he said 'oh, and you're doing okay now?' 'Yeah, I'm doing great.' 'Well,' he said, 'would you like to stay here?' Hah! 'Well,' I says, 'I was going to ask you exactly that same question… I would love to stay here. That's what I – I fell in love with the place.' 'Well', he says, 'it's people like you that we'd like to get here. By the way,' he says, 'my name is Angus Chisholm and originally I'm from Inverness in Scotland'. Oh, so I was in good hands there.*[23]

Highland networking, both with Angus Chisholm and with Oban-born Iain MacTavish, personnel manager of a Vancouver shipping company, helped Murdo to secure employment with a Vancouver shipping company. He later moved on to the Vancouver Fire Department, in whose service he remained for thirty-five years, working mostly on fire boats in the harbour, before he retired in 1991. He met his Acharacle-born wife at a ceilidh at the Scottish Auditorium and for more than five decades he has maintained strong links with his Hebridean roots.

> *Now I was going to say when I first came here I was really surprised at how many people that was here from the Outer Hebrides. There was eleven people from that little village of Arnol staying in Vancouver at that time and myself being*

number twelve. And I went up to visit – the second year I was here, in 54, I went up to Trail to visit a first cousin of mine that was living in Trail that had come out in 1929, and there was I think 14 people from Arnol between Trail and Proctor.... And I was just amazed at the amount of people that was from that little village in that – in this part of the world in British Columbia. It was really really nice to meet all those people and hear their stories. But I had heard some of the stories while I was growing up because quite a few of the people that used to come to our house and talk about their experiences in the army and in the navy and in South America and Canada and Australia and a lot of them had gone home after being out here, sometimes before the First World War and aft – they went home in the early 30s at the beginning of the Depression because there was, there was no jobs and stuff, so they went back home. And I heard about the Kootenay Lakes and the coast of British Columbia when I was 5, 6, 7, 8, 9, 10 years old so I was – felt quite at home here from the first day I landed here, and I have not regretted even for two minutes that I came here.[24]

Issues of Identity

A Hebridean identity can be maintained or reconfigured overseas. When Morag Bennett arrived in Canada, she was a monolingual Gaelic speaker, and in conversation she recalled in passing her wish to blend in with the other children.

We all spoke Gaelic to each other, so I heard it, and my mother and father spoke Gaelic to each other too, in the house. We went to school then, and of course, we wanted to be like the other children, and we didn't think much of the Gaelic language at that particular stage.[25]

At the age of ninety-one, she declared that she still thought in Gaelic, even though she no longer had the opportunity to speak the language. A generation later, Murdo Macivor made a conscious effort to maintain his first language, and he and his late wife were both leading members of the Gaelic Society of Vancouver.

The church was another institution that for many generations facilitated the retention of ethnic identity among emigrants, as well as helping them to develop social networks and find a job. Hundreds of ministers from all parts of Scotland went to the colonies and dominions to pastor Scottish churches. One such was the Reverend Roderick MacKenzie from Lochs, who in 1924 found his last resting place at Cape North, in the far north of Cape Breton Island. After training at Glasgow University and then at New College in Edinburgh, MacKenzie went to Canada in 1904, where he ministered to Scottish expatriates in three different charges. After eight years at Winslow in the Eastern Townships of Quebec he went to Strathlorne in Cape Breton, and in 1919 to Cape North.[26] Much earlier, in 1817, the defrocked minister Norman McLeod from Assynt had set sail from Ullapool with 400 followers, in the famous Odyssey of the so-called 'Normanites'. Their worldwide wanderings took them first to Pictou in Nova Scotia, then to St Ann's in Cape Breton, and ultimately, via Adelaide and Melbourne, to their final destination at Waipu in New Zealand's North Island. The town's cemetery – located in a landscape reminiscent of the Assynt district from which many of them or their ancestors had come – records the Hebridean and west highland origins of emigrants who had left Scotland for Canada but had ended their pilgrimage on the other side of the world, where in 1851 they reconstituted a 1,000-strong Gaelic-speaking community.[27]

Conclusion: Continuities and Changes

What are the recurring and changing characteristics of Hebridean emigration throughout the centuries that have been covered both in this paper and in the wider conference of which it is a part? One frequently recurring refrain is public distaste for emigration. That in turn is firmly bound up with the exilic theme so commonly associated with the Hebridean exodus, even though – as has been demonstrated – many individual participants were consciously entrepreneurial. Another continuing theme is the centrality of recruitment agents to both decision making and organization, as well as the polarized reactions to their activities. They were always controversial figures, whether they were eighteenth-century military recruiters, land colonizers such as the Earl of Selkirk, Australian bounty agents such as Dr David Boyter in the 1830s, or professional appointees of the dominion governments who swarmed across the country from the 1870s. Networking and chain migration were also of inestimable importance in stimulating and sustaining an exodus, and many emigrants had a preliminary awareness of the land to which they were going – particularly if it was North America – because of the volume and impact of letters and return visits by those who had preceded them.

Among the changes associated with the emigration process the onward march of technology must rank among the most important. While emigrants had always come and gone, perhaps most notably in the fur trade, ever improving communications speeded up the exchange of news and made serial and return movement much easier. It also helped to engender 'roots tourism' in both donor and host nations, and indeed, perhaps the construction of a tourist industry built at least partly on a fascination with victimhood is the ultimate example of how exile has been turned into entrepreneurship.[28] Nova Scotia initiated a 'tartanizing' process as early as the 1930s, in a deliberate attempt to revitalize the province's ailing economy by trading on its Scottish heritage.[29] It was also in the 1930s that transatlantic shipping companies began to capitalize on the commercial potential of the homecoming holidaymaking highlander, a potential which has enjoyed its coming-of-age in 2009, Scotland's official Year of Homecoming.

Notes

1. Mary McKerrow, *The Faeds: a biography* (Edinburgh: Canongate, 1982), 110–11; Duncan Macmillan, *Scottish Art: 1460–2000* (Edinburgh: Mainstream, 2000), 105–6, 217–18; Peter McEwan, *Dictionary of Scottish Art and Architecture* (Woodbridge, Suffolk: Antique Collectors' Club, 1994), 529; http://www.scran.ac.uk/database/record.php?usi=000-000-579-758C&scache=27szwoxnq9&searchdb=scran
2. For a selection of photographs, see Jim Wilkie, *Metagama: a journey from Lewis to the New World* (Edinburgh: Birlinn, 2001, originally published 1987).
3. Samuel Johnson, *A Journey to the Western Islands of Scotland*, edited by R. W. Chapman (Oxford: Oxford University Press, 1984), 87.
4. *The Statistical Account of Scotland, 1791–99*, vol. 13, p. 317, North Uist, County of Inverness. http://stat-acc-scot.edina.ac.uk/link/1791-99/Inverness/North%20Uist/
5. Marjory Harper, *Adventurers and Exiles: the great Scottish exodus* (London: Profile, 2004), 117–19.
6. James Boswell, *The Journal of a Tour to the Hebrides with Samuel Johnson* (London, 1786), edited by R. W. Chapman (Oxford: Oxford University Press, 1984), 346.

7. Eric Richards, *The Highland Clearances: people, landlords and rural turmoil* (Edinburgh: Birlinn, 2000), 217–24. The quotation from the eyewitness is on page 220. See also T. M. Devine, *The Great Highland Famine: hunger, emigration and the Scottish Highlands in the nineteenth century* (Edinburgh: John Donald, 1988), ch. 8.
8. Quoted in Richards, *The Highland Clearances*, 2.
9. National Archives of Scotland, RH 1/2/612/9, Adam Hope, London, Upper Canada to George Hope, Fenton Barns, Haddington, 8 October 1849.
10. Wayne Norton, *Help us to a Better Land: crofter colonies in the prairie West* (Regina: Canadian Plains Research Center, 1994).
11. Library and Archives Canada, MG 27, C-1352 1L 1B5, The Journal of Lady Aberdeen (unpublished), 7 October 1890.
12. National Archives of Scotland, AF51/198/514, Lawlor to Sir George Trevelyan, 21 January 1895.
13. PP 1884, XXXII–XXXVI, *Report of HM Commissioners of Inquiry into the Condition of the Crofters and Cottars in the Highlands and Islands of Scotland*, Appendix A, XXXII, 125–6. Emigration from the Long Island. Letters of emigrants from the property of Lady Gordon Cathcart.
14. Marjory Harper, *Emigration from Scotland between the Wars: opportunity or exile?* (Manchester: Manchester University Press, 1998), 6–7.
15. For details see The Scottish Emigration Database, www.abdn.ac.uk/emigration
16. John Macleod, *When I Heard the Bell: the loss of the* Iolaire (Edinburgh: Birlinn, 2009).
17. For details on the Empire Settlement Act, and its implications for Scottish emigration, see Harper, *Emigration from Scotland between the Wars*, 17–27.
18. For a full discussion of the 1923 emigrations from the Outer Hebrides, see Marjory Harper, 'Crofter colonists in Canada: an experiment in empire settlement in the 1920s', *Northern*

Scotland, 14 (1994), 69–108. For details on the *Metagama* emigrants, see Wilkie, *Metagama*.

19. Author's interview with Morag Bennett, 21 February 2005.
20. NSW Bicentennial Oral History Project, interview no. 137, Angus McDonald interviewed by Paula Hamilton, 1 September 1987.
21. Author's interview with Calum, Cathie and Chrissie Murray, 25 February 2005.
22. *Ibid.*
23. Author's interview with Murdo Macivor, 7 December 2007.
24. *Ibid.*
25. Author's interview with Morag Bennett, 21 February 2005.
26. John Murray, *The History of the Presbyterian Church in Cape Breton* (Truro, NS: np, 1921), 130.
27. There are many books on the history of the 'Normanites'. See, *inter alia*, Flora McPherson, *Watchman against the World: the remarkable journey of Norman McLeod & his people from Scotland to Cape Breton Island to New Zealand* (Wreck Cove, NS: Breton Books, 1993) and Neil C. Robinson, *Lion of Scotland* (Edinburgh: Birlinn, 1999, originally published 1952).
28. For an evaluation of roots tourism see Paul Basu, 'Roots tourism as return movement: semantics and the Scottish diaspora' in Marjory Harper (ed.), *Emigrant Homecomings: the return movement of emigrants, 1600–2000* (Manchester: Manchester University Press, 2005), 131–52.
29. Ian McKay, 'Tartanism triumphant: the construction of Scottishness in Nova Scotia, 1933–1954', *Acadiensis*, XXI, 2 (Spring 1992), 5–47.

Close of Conference Address

Michael Russell MSP, Minister for Culture, External Affairs and the Constitution

Introduction

Feasgar math a' Chairdean

Tha mi glè thoilichte a bhith comhla ruibh an diugh. Bha mi a' fuireach anns na h-Eileanan seo airson beagan bliadhnachan agus tha mi an còmhnaidh tolichte le cothrom a bhith air ais a rithist.

[*Good afternoon friends, I am very pleased to be with you today. I stayed in these islands for a few years and I am always pleased with the opportunity to be back again.*]

It has been a great pleasure to take part in the Island Emigrants event.

Prominent Island Themes

There are many prominent themes in the history of these Scottish islands. As we are aware the main themes are probably land, belief, language, culture and of course emigration.

These themes are not new, but have been prominent for the last couple of centuries and these concerns are still reflected in our political debate, in our literature and in the writing of our history. Even this morning, much of the debate has centred on these themes in terms of identity.

The focus of this event is Island Emigrants and I believe it is fitting that this event should be held here. Emigration is a key theme in Scottish history, but I expect this subject and its implications are more keenly felt in these islands.

These Islands

I expect it is also in these islands that the associated family and community links remain and are best maintained. This is not new as the themes of clearance and emigration have been prominent in the consciousness of island communities for generations and long before current historical interest.

I welcome the added interest and focus that has been brought to this by our Homecoming celebrations. And the unique invitation Scotland has given to the world this year – this is the first time Scotland has issued a co-ordinated invitation to welcome our global family home.

Diaspora

Homecoming has done much to reconnect Scotland with the estimated tens of millions of people worldwide who claim Scottish ancestry. Many of them will be able to trace their roots back to these islands.

And I would like to thank the many speakers over the last few days all of whom help to maintain these connections and make them more than just numbers or words – who keep the connections real and personal.

And we in the Scottish Government recognise the importance and value of maintaining connections with our Diaspora.

Beyond the Homecoming celebrations, we will continue to work with and strengthen relationships for the benefit of Scotland and all Scots, whether here in Scotland, or first generation ex-pats or those who can trace their family heritage back to Scotland through centuries.

The people and families that emigrated from the Western Isles would of course have been Gaelic speaking and this drain of people, along with other factors, has had an effect on the strength of Gaelic in Scotland.

Gaelic

Gaelic has had a difficult history over the last century. The Scottish Government is, however, committed to taking the necessary action to create a new generation of Gaelic speakers in Scotland. This Government's aim is to see a secure and sustainable future for Gaelic in Scotland.

The only way we can deliver this is to increase the number of people using Gaelic in everyday life. We aim to reassess our current Gaelic activities and priorities and establish a range of ambitious outcomes that we recognise will achieve this in relation to Gaelic.

In this an increase of Gaelic speakers will sit at the top of our agenda and our most urgent and pressing need is to focus our energies on the steps we need to take to achieve this.

In connection with this, I would like to thank the members of the Islands Book Trust, not only for reflecting the diversity of these islands in their publications list but in continuing to do this in Gaelic and English. 'Cum ort'.

Culture

And of course the Trust organises events like this, events which celebrate our heritage, our language and our culture.

The fun, fulfilment and creative stimulation of taking part in culture, the arts and heritage activity are valued by many individuals and communities across Scotland. Audiences and participants alike find these experiences add substantially to their lives.

We know that this is true in the islands, as in the Scottish mainland – culture is valued highly and commitment to it is strong.

Great Book of Gaelic

Our language and our culture provide Scotland with a unique voice with which to reach out to our global family, to keep us connected.

Over the last few days, this conference has focused on the many people that have left these islands and settled in other parts of the world. As we know, family and community links still exist and in many cases are strong and healthy.

These links and the exchanges that follow between communities here and overseas carry the potential to enrich the cultural life of both Scotland and overseas communities.

One recent initiative that has the potential to strengthen links and enrich cultural life is the Great Book of Gaelic which is currently touring North America. I have been a strong supporter of this project and I am confident it has the potential to strengthen cultural ties at this time.

The exhibition will soon be opening in Sydney, Cape Breton then Port Hawkesbury and after that Antigonish.

I believe it is important for the Scottish Government to demonstrate our practical support for initiatives such as these. We have identified some funding with which we can support the travelling exhibition and the associated programme and I will look forward to hearing reports of its progress.

Homecoming

I hope that you have all had the opportunity to participate in and enjoy the Homecoming celebrations so far. An evaluation of Homecoming is being undertaken and the results of this will be available following the close of the celebration but there are many positive indicators that show that the celebration is already a success and well on its way to meeting its targets. With nearly 400 fantastic events, festivals and activities taking place the length and breadth of the country and in every local authority area that does not come as a surprise.

Your conference here has been a great addition to the Homecoming programme and I wish you the best in each of the future celebrations of your Scottish culture and roots.